Ed – Thank you for being here.
It was great getting to know y
Wish you the Best in y
— Marcie

Ed,
Thank you for supporting us through this transition.
Best of luck to you in the future! Stay in touch.
— Chico

Ed,
You are a
legend, it was
an honor to
learn from you
Stephen Roberts

Thank you!

Ed – you came &
showed us the way
at a crucial time
in our company.
We say thank u!

To my fellow alum,
Thanks for your
help & Good luck on
what's next!
Ed Doug

Ed,
Thank you for supporting
our IT department during a
difficult time.
We truly appreciate you!
Best wishes
Susan

Best wishes Ed! ☺
Robin

Ed –
Thanks for your
and supporting
TRIO IT. Best wishes
Noelle

Ed, thank you
for supporting
TRINITY! I wish
you the best!
— Cade

Thank you for serving as the
ringleader of our three ring circus!
It was a pleasure getting to know you
and hope our paths cross again
some day.
— Dauson

THE LEGEND OF
TRINITY
INDUSTRIES, INC.

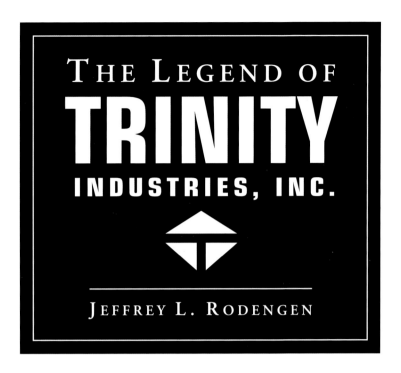

THE LEGEND OF
TRINITY
INDUSTRIES, INC.

JEFFREY L. RODENGEN

Edited by Alex Lieber
Design and layout by Jill Apolinario & Rachelle Donley

For Jacques Dorgambide,
chevalier and bon ami.

Also by Jeff Rodengen

The Legend of Chris-Craft

IRON FIST: The Lives
of Carl Kiekhaefer

Evinrude-Johnson and
The Legend of OMC

Serving the Silent Service:
The Legend of Electric Boat

The Legend of Dr Pepper/Seven-Up

The Legend of Honeywell

The Legend of Briggs & Stratton

The Legend of Ingersoll-Rand

The MicroAge Way

The Legend of Stanley:
150 Years of The Stanley Works

The Legend of Halliburton

The Legend of
York International

The Legend of Nucor Corporation

The Legend of Goodyear:
The First 100 Years

The Legend of AMP

The Legend of Cessna

The Legend of VF Corporation

The Spirit of AMD

The Legend of Rowan

New Horizons:
The Story of Ashland Inc.

The History of
American Standard

The Legend of Mercury Marine

The Legend of Federal-Mogul

Against the Odds:
Inter-Tel—The First 30 Years

The Legend of Pfizer

State of the Heart: The Practical Guide
to Your Heart and Heart Surgery
with Larry W. Stephenson, M.D.

The Legend of Worthington Industries

Publisher's Cataloging in Publication

Rodengen, Jeffrey L.
    The legend of Trinity /Jeffrey L. Rodengen. – 1st ed.
    p. cm.
    Includes bibliographical references and index.
    ISBN 0-945903-53-7

    1. Trinity Industries, Inc. – History. 2. Railroad equipment
industry – United States – History. 3. Pipe fittings industry –
United States – History. 4. Concrete products industry – United
States – History. I. Title.

HD9712.U54R64 2000
338.7/62524/0973   QBI99-1322

Write Stuff Enterprises, Inc.
1001 South Andrews Avenue, Second Floor • Fort Lauderdale, FL 33316
1-800-900-Book (1-800-900-2665) • (954) 462-6657
www.writestuffbooks.com

Library of Congress Catalog Card Number 99-71036
ISBN 0-945903-53-7

Completely produced in the United States of America
10 9 8 7 6 5 4 3 2 1

TABLE OF CONTENTS

INTRODUCTION

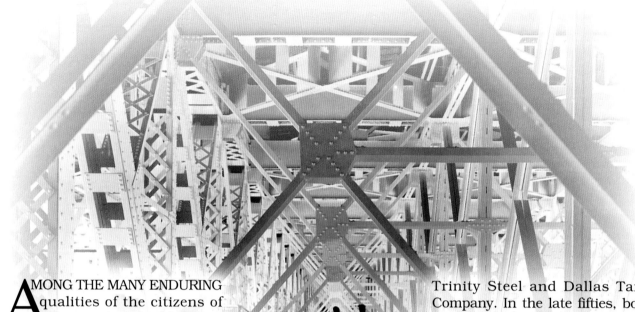

AMONG THE MANY ENDURING qualities of the citizens of the great state of Texas, two stand out: a pioneering spirit and an unshakable faith in a vision of the future. It was these qualities that led Sam Houston and a small army of determined settlers to overcome overwhelming odds and pave the way for eventual statehood. And it was these qualities that have built Texas into the 11th largest economy in the world.

This spirit of building for the future when others withdraw to await more certain times continues in the modern form of our most successful business enterprises. Among the best examples of this is Trinity Industries, a company whose Texan roots are now spread throughout the world under the leadership of Tim Wallace and his management team.

Wallace, a 25-year-veteran of Trinity, succeeded his father W. Ray Wallace as chairman and CEO in 1998. As the third chairman and second CEO of this global corporation, Tim is carrying on a proud legacy by ensuring that Trinity is the finest and most efficient company in the markets it serves. He and his team are determined to make Trinity the best place to work while producing strong financial results and continued growth.

Trinity traces its roots to two Dallas manufacturers of liquefied petroleum gas (LPG) tanks:

Trinity Steel and Dallas Tank Company. In the late fifties, both were struggling to survive in a market choked by competition.

Trinity Steel was where Ray Wallace got his start as employee number 17. Ray had been lured from California by his uncle, a master salesman and industrious visionary by the name of C.J. Bender, the man who founded the original Trinity in a small mule barn. C.J. knew how tough the competition was, and he knew what was needed to give Trinity the edge.

C.J. needed someone with engineering expertise so he gave his nephew a call. Fresh from the oil fields of California, Ray signed on as an engineer, but he soon became fluent in all aspects of the business. His salary at the time was a princely $225 a month; Ray believed that if he worked hard he might someday earn the royal sum of $500 a month.

In 1958, Trinity and Dallas Tank agreed to join forces. The reborn company soon became one of the leading manufacturers of steel tanks and pressure vessels in the nation.

When Trinity and Dallas Tank merged, Ray was selected to lead the new organization. His vision was simple: to survive, Trinity had to grow. To grow Trinity, he would take advantage of a variety of market opportunities. Ray continuously identified good companies that had fallen on hard times, bought them up for pennies on the dollar and then turned them into profitable enterprises.

Trinity's product diversity grew by cascading into a series of steel fabrication businesses. One such area was the railcar market. The company began by producing LPG containers and then grew into larger tanks, tankcar barrels, hopper bodies, but then expanded into building the complete railcar. When railcar production plummeted in the mid-eighties, Ray launched a strategy of purchasing disillusioned and failing competitors, including legendary Pullman Standard, which dominated the industry for years. Naysayers doubted the wisdom of investing so much in idle plants and rusting equipment. They failed to appreciate the entrepreneurial vision of planning for the eventual — and overdue — replacement of America's rolling stock.

Trinity also pursued a bold strategy in the marine and construction segments, buying such venerable companies as Mosher Steel, whose products form the backbone of New York's World Trade Center, and Equitable Shipyards, which pioneered the *Frank Phillips*, the oil industry's first offshore location and supply barge. For the first time, a crew could work and sleep on the location of an offshore oil well. The *Phillips*, incidentally, brought in the first offshore oil well out of the sight of land.

Trinity boasted a product line that ran the gamut of steel products — railcars, barges, steel products for the construction industry and highway guardrails — steel products that could be shaped and worked into a profitable commodity. Along the way, it has consistently proved the critics wrong. In the 1990s, the company was criticized when it entered the concrete aggregates market. Trinity, they said, had no business straying into non-steel products. Less than nine years later Trinity has become one of the largest concrete, sand and aggregate producers in the state of Texas.

In July 1998, after 52 years with the same company, and 40 as its chief executive, Ray Wallace stepped aside and Tim Wallace took the reins. Like his father, Tim gathered a corporate team together to chart a new future for Trinity Industries. In this global, information-driven economy, Tim and his team are transforming Trinity into a diversified industrial company that continues its focus on growth, one that attracts and retains the best and the brightest by offering an endless stream of opportunities.

Today, Trinity can be truly proud of its many accomplishments and of the contributions it has made to the transportation, marine, construction and industrial products industries throughout the United States and the world. With operations in 20 states and four countries, Trinity employs more than 17,500 employees in 75 facilities and generates revenues approaching $3 billion. Continuing a pioneering legacy of imagination and vision, like Texas' founding citizens, Trinity has consistently met the challenges of survival against the odds, often against the advice of those whose names are now forgotten

ACKNOWLEDGMENTS

A GREAT MANY INDIVIDUALS and institutions assisted in the research, preparation and publication of *The Legend of Trinity.*

Much of the principal archival research was accomplished by the talented and dedicated research assistant, Joan Thompson. Her thorough and careful work made it possible to publish much new and interesting information about the origins of Trinity Industries.

Without the generous assistance of scores of Trinity executives, employees and retirees, this book would have been impossible to produce. All reached back in their memories and offered fascinating personal accounts that have enriched the story immeasurably.

I would like to especially thank Tim Wallace, chairman and CEO of Trinity, and his father, Ray Wallace, chairman emeritus. Both are amazing individuals who possess remarkable memories. Their contributions were indispensable.

A number of individuals were also extremely helpful. In particular, Dick Martin provided invaluable assistance, often on short notice, to ensure the accuracy of the timeline. I would also like to thank Graceanna Jones for helping pull the final pieces of the book together, and Trinna Dean for her cheerful assistance.

Many executives, past and present, enriched the book with their perspectives. Among these I would like to thank John Adams, Norman Adams, Buddy Alexander, John W. Banks, Ralph Banks, Bill Barnett, Tom Blissett, Don Bodinger, Ed Boulter, Ed Breeding, Richard Brown, Manuel Castro, Wally Cathcart, Jack Cunningham, Tom Fortunato, Sue Gibbons, Don Graham, Wayne Hacker, Jess Hay, Don Hestand, Keith Hittle, Edmund Hoffman, Robert Hursted, Helmut Hvizdalek, Jim Ivy, Bob Kenney, Todd Lokash, Lee McElroy, Bill Neewby, John Nussrallah, Joe Piriano, Doug Schneider, Steve Smith, Cecil Spear, Oscar Stewart and Mark Stiles.

A number of Trinity's customers were also extremely helpful. They provided an "outsider's insight" into the company's history. Among these I would like to thank Ray Burton, chairman and CEO of TTX; Ward Fuller, president of GATX; Matt Rose, president and COO of Burlington Northern Sante Fe; and Reuben Perin, retired vice president of U.S. Steel.

Grateful thanks are also due to Don Banks. Banks generously lent a great number of images that made it possible to illustrate the history of Dallas Tank.

A number of institutions were also very helpful in providing images. Their staffs were often asked to find and reproduce images on short notice. They responded with the utmost courtesy and professionalism. I am grateful to Anne Calhoun, of the B&O Railroad Museum; Ellen Roberts, of the Butler County Historical Society; Wayne Everard, of the New Orleans Public Library; Baylor Media Services; the California State Railroad Museum; and the Greenville Historical Society.

Finally, a special word of thanks to the hardworking staff at Write Stuff. Proofreader Bonnie Freeman, transcriptionist Mary Aaron and indexer Erica Orloff worked quickly and efficiently.

Particular thanks go to David Patten, author/executive, who conducted many valuable interviews. I also extend appreciation to Alex Lieber, executive editor; Jon VanZile and Melody Maysonet, associate editors; Colleen Azcona and Amanda Fowler, executive assistants; Sandy Cruz, senior art director; Rachelle Donley, Jill Apolinario and Dennis Shockley, art directors; Fred Moll, production manager; Marianne Roberts, office manager; Mike Monahan, director of marketing; Rafael Santiago, logistics specialist; and Karine Rodengen, project coordinator.

In 1940, homes used about a billion gallons of liquefied petroleum gas each year. In the fifties, residential use topped a billion gallons each month.

CHAPTER ONE

PROUD DREAMS

"You know I'm not going to fire you, and I know you're not going to quit."

— C.J. Bender to nephew W. Ray Wallace, 1946[1]

IN 1946, C.J. BENDER PUT HIS arm around Trinity Steel's newest employee, nephew Ray Wallace, outside the drafty mule barn that served as the company's shop and predicted, "We're going to build something. One day, you'll be proud of what we're going to have."[2]

Wallace responded that he was already proud of what he had learned from his uncle and what they had accomplished. C.J. waved the response aside. "Oh, no, we haven't got anything compared to what we're going to have," Wallace recalled Bender saying. "But there's one thing that we can both be a whole lot more comfortable with each other about: You know I'm not going to fire you, and I know you're not going to quit."[3]

What C.J. said that day came true. By the time Wallace retired 52 years later, Trinity was one of North America's largest manufacturers of transportation, construction and industrial products with more than $2.4 billion in revenue. It had more than 12 million square feet of manufacturing space in 78 plants spread across 22 states, as well as Mexico and Brazil.

Trinity Industries had its beginnings in the merger of two companies, Trinity Steel and its more established competitor, Dallas Tank (see Chapter Two). Bender founded Trinity Steel Company on July 1, 1944. He joined with two brothers, Roger and Thomas Tennant, to launch a company that made transport and storage tanks for butane and liquefied petroleum gas (LPG). This relatively new fuel source was quickly becoming popular. Bender, who owned 40 percent of the business, worked out of the barn at 513 South Hill Avenue in Dallas.[4]

Bender and his partners possessed different temperaments, which led to frequent infighting over business strategy.[5] Their verbal battles were rancorous and bitter, so much so that the constant feuding left Bender physically ill. His wife, fearing for his health, told him to see his friend, Dr. W. Howard Bryant, in Tyler. A good doctor, Bryant recommended a cure. He offered to become the best kind of partner with Bender — a silent one.[6]

Their partnership began on July 5, 1946. After they bought out the other partners, Bender held 75 percent ownership and Bryant owned 25 percent.[7] Although he was relieved of the arguments, Bender now faced another problem. With the Tennants' departure Bender lost the company's engineering expertise. He found himself wondering "now what am I going to do" because he did not know how to actually build the products. Bender was a salesman.[8]

Trinity Steel was named for the Trinity River, which runs from Dallas to Galveston Bay. C.J. Bender founded the company with two partners in 1944.

C.J. Bender was a consummate salesman. He always saw the importance of promoting his products' features.

C.J. Bender: Portrait of a Salesman

Charles Jonathan Bender, known universally as C.J., grew up in Colorado. A devoted family man, he married Fina Belle, whom he nicknamed "Chummy" because she was not only his wife but his chum.[9]

Bender was a wonderfully prolific storyteller with a passion for such outdoor recreations as fishing and farming. An avid hunter, he was a founder of the One Shot Antelope Hunt in Wyoming. Bender and his friends once headed to Africa on hunting trips and returned with "edge-of-your-seat" stories of his adventures.[10]

He carried this same sense of competition and energy into his business relationships. One of his favorite expressions was, "If every one of our competitors were laid end to end, it would serve them right."[11] But C.J. Bender was foremost a

salesman, displaying that rare and vital quality of all successful salesmen: He used every experience as a learning tool. He learned, for instance, the importance of selling on features while he was managing an automobile dealership in San Antonio. Lathering up to shave one day, Bender spotted a brand new Essex automobile in his neighbor's driveway. Furious, C.J. walked over to his neighbor's house and said, "What on earth! You bought a new Essex and you know I'm selling Pontiacs, and we've been friends living next door to each other four years now."[12]

His friend explained the reason, which Bender would pass on to Ray Wallace years later:

> *"Well, C.J., ... I'm about 6 feet 2 inches tall, and Mary is only about 5 feet 3 inches, and every time she tried to drive the car, we just had to have a whole pile of pillows to get her there. But the Essex has a new deal they invented to move this seat up. It just suits her, and I can move it back and drive comfortably. That's why we bought this car."[13]*

C.J. was astounded. Pontiac had invented the sliding seat mechanism, but Essex had done a better job of promoting the feature. He told his friend, "Why, hell, we invented the thing!"[14]

Bender always remembered the gentle yet scathing answer: "Well, C.J., you never told me that."

From that moment on, Bender never failed to incorporate features into his sales pitch. "He sold each little nut and screw and item on there as though it was the only tank in the country that had it," said Wallace.[15] When selling a particular line of tanks later, Bender expounded on the easy-to-read gauge. A photograph at a sales convention displayed a cutout of a tank with the large gauge. The salesman standing nearby even wore a suit with a replica of a gauge pinned to his jacket.

These early tanks were a major product line for Trinity as LPG established itself as an important home-fuel source. In the late 1930s, Bender had first heard about LPG as an odorless, petroleum-based product that became liquid under pressure, making it a clean-burning fuel source that was easier to transport than butane, which was the industry standard.[16] Bender began selling LP tanks on consignment and did such a brisk business he left car sales. "I got to a point to where I felt selling

CHAPTER ONE: PROUD DREAMS

tanks was easier than selling cars," he noted. "I finally gave up selling cars, which I'd sold all my life. I thought, well, if I can sell these tanks, why don't I figure out how to build these dang things?"[17]

Bender never looked back at the car business. He often said that "a bad day in the steel business is a lot better than a good day in the car business." It was a lesson driven home to both Ray Wallace and later his son, Tim Wallace.[18]

But building things had never been his strong suit. Starting a modest company he called Automatic Gas Equipment (later merged with Trinity Steel), he learned how to put the finish-

ing touches on manufactured butane tanks meant for underground storage. He painted them, wrapped them in burlap and screwed on valves before covering the fittings with hoods.[19] He gradually absorbed a working knowledge of the tanks but could never have been called an engineer. So when he parted ways with his original partners, Bender knew he needed someone he could count on. That was when he called his nephew Ray and offered him a job.

W. Ray Wallace

W. Ray Wallace was born in Shreveport, Louisiana, on March 25, 1923, the son of Jason Mahoney Wallace and Mattie Evelyn Adair Wallace. Although Ray was born in Louisiana, he had Texas roots. His family had been in Texas since 1855, when Ray's grandfather, Finis Ray "F.R." Wallace, came to the Lone Star state.

In what would become a familiar trait in the Wallace clan, F.R. Wallace had earned a reputation

Above left: The full-sized cutaway of a propane tank shows the advanced features of the increased flow capacity valves and the easy-to-read float gauge.

Below: A load of underground butane tanks. C.J. Bender started out in the business by finishing tanks.

as one of the most enterprising farmers in his county. According to *A History of Texas*, F.R. began freighting goods when he was 16. He was extremely resourceful, even at that young age. On his trips, F.R. occasionally broke an axle on his wagon. Undeterred, "he would cut a piece of timber from a neighboring wood and with only what tools he happened to have along with him would make another axle and proceed on his way."[20] Through the years, F.R. Wallace dabbled in many other businesses. At various times, he ran a hotel with a feed stable, operated a brickworks and opened a drugstore. He also dealt in cattle and mules, as well as being "engaged to some extent as a dealer in farm machinery, threshers, hay-presses, etc. (The larger portion of his right hand had been torn by a threshing machine.)"[21] He and his first wife, who died in 1886, had three children, including Jason Mahoney Wallace. Fina Belle Wallace, the future wife of C.J. Bender, was born from F.R. Wallace's second marriage.

Jason Wallace died when his son, Ray, was only $1\frac{1}{2}$. At the time, Ray's mother was pregnant with a daughter, Memory Jo. After Memory Jo was born, Mattie Wallace's mother moved in to help take care of the two children while Mattie worked as an executive secretary at the electric company. Ray Wallace recalled that "I didn't realize the difference in our standard of living as compared to the kids I grew up with until much later in my life when it occurred to me how my mother was able to manage our finances with just one income."[22]

The Wallace work ethic was strongly instilled in Ray. In fact, his uncle worried about Ray's lack of interest in hobbies. In later years Bender complained to his great-nephew, Tim Wallace, saying, "I give your father golf clubs. I give him fishing poles. I give him guns, and ... he doesn't do anything but work.... I keep saying, 'Ray, you just got to learn to have some fun.'"[23]

Wallace graduated from Louisiana Tech with a degree in civil engineering in 1944. Getting through college hadn't been easy. A major car accident five years earlier had left him with four steel plates in his arm and a mountain of hospital bills. When he wasn't in class, Wallace worked to pay off the debt by taking a variety of jobs, from busboy to surveyor. But he knew he was one of the lucky ones; one of his friends had died in the crash.

Bender stressed the importance of selling features. Here, Ray Wallace points out the easy-to-read gauge fitted on Trinity Steel's tanks.

After college, Wallace worked for the Austin Bridge Company in Dallas, performing drafting work and acting as assistant to the superintendent. In spite of his college education, Wallace was not making enough money, and he seriously thought of going to Alaska "because there was big money there, and I was, at that point, needing to make more money and get shed of some debt."[24]

With Alaska as his goal, Wallace became a core analyst in 1945 for Core Laboratories, an oilfield service company located in Bakersfield, California. He believed he could earn enough money there to pay his way to Alaska and seek his fortune.

Wallace worked at Core Laboratories for nearly two years. "They had a laboratory that was mounted on a ton-and-a-half truck, and you'd go alongside the oil well and they'd pull cores ... out of the well, and then we would analyze them right on the spot," he said. "We had a trailer that we pulled along that we slept in."[25] The job involved stretches of down time followed by round-the-clock work, he remembered. "We could go weeks, two or three weeks, and never do a lick of work, and then we'd work 48 or 50 hours straight without stopping and take off for six or eight hours and do it again."[26]

Wallace was able to pay off his old debts, but then came a call from Bender, who asked his nephew to return to Dallas and work for him as an engineer. Wallace hesitated. He would have to give up the Alaskan dream. He said he wanted to

give notice to his employers first, but Bender needed a decision immediately: "I need somebody now. I need you now. I need an engineer."[27]

On August 1, 1946, Wallace became the 17th employee at Trinity Steel. He was paid the princely sum of $225 a month, up from the $190 a month he had made in California. Although his official title was engineer, "there wasn't enough to keep you busy as an engineer, so I swept the floor and loaded the tanks. At that moment in time, I was in hopes that someday I would make $500 a month."[28]

Life at Trinity

Wallace's first task was to figure out how to make tanks out of the oddball lengths of steel the company had mistakenly purchased. Bender complained the metal for the shell plate, when rolled, was too short in the circumference and would not match the ends of the tanks.[29] He wanted his nephew to fix the problem. After talking with the workers, Wallace said they found the solution.

"Because the one steel plate was too short, the solution was to weld two steel plates together to obtain the proper circumferential length. After the steel plate was rolled, it matched the ends of the tank perfectly. Bender thought this was pure genius because he had been told the steel plates could never be used, and a lot of money had been tied up in those plates."[30]

Trinity had been making butane tanks with diameters ranging between 24 inches and 30 inches and lengths averaging about seven feet to eight feet. Its customers included butane gas dealers who sold the equipment in rural areas not served by natural gas pipelines. The tanks were painted to prevent corrosion and were installed underground. They supplied vapors, burned as gas, to heat homes, water and food.

Six months after Wallace arrived at Trinity, the company acquired the business of Bender's other company, the Automatic Gas Equipment

Ray Wallace, far left, was hired as an engineer but also became a salesman for Trinity.

LPG–A NEW KIND OF FUEL

LIQUEFIED PETROLEUM GAS, KNOWN AS LPG, is composed of butane, propane or a combination of both. The gas turns to liquid under moderate pressure, making it possible to move or store in pressurized containers. Today, LPG can be used as a heating and cooking fuel, as raw material for the chemical and petrochemical industries and as fuel for equipment such as forklifts.

The LPG industry was born on May 17, 1912, when, according to the trade magazine *LPGA Times*, liquefied petroleum "began lighting the lamps and cooking the meals in the farm home of John Gahring" near Waterford, Pennsylvania.[1] Gahring was the first customer of American Gasol Company, cofounded by Dr. Walter O. Snelling, pictured at right, a chemist with the federal Bureau of Mines.

Snelling, who held degrees from Harvard, Yale and George Washington universities, is credited with the commercial development of propane and butane for use as domestic fuels.[2] He began searching for an alternative to gasoline in 1910, after a man walked into his Pittsburgh office, angry because the gasoline for his car evaporated too quickly, and he wanted someone in the government to find out why. According to a history in *LPGA Times*, "[Snelling] soon realized that gases were escaping from the liquid gasoline.

"Experimenting with the fuel and checking the nature of its components, Dr. Snelling realized he had butane, propane and other hydrocarbons to deal with. Since there were no facilities for preparing the various frac-

tions of his sample fuel, Dr. Snelling, having mechanical as well as chemical skills, set about building a distilling apparatus."[3]

Snelling used coils from an old hot water heater and pieces of laboratory equipment to build a still that separated gasoline into its liquid and gaseous components.

His device was successful, but the market for LPG did not take off, in part because of high production and distribution costs. More than 20 years would pass after the first use before the commercial possibilities of LPG were realized, which happened when "a large productive capacity and a matching market potential would stimulate serious efforts by a few large companies to develop the LP-Gas fuel industry."[4]

Indeed, the production did boom in the 1920s, doubling from 465,000 gallons in 1926 to 1.1 million gallons only a year later and then quadrupling to 4.5 million gallons in 1928, according to the Bureau of Mines.[5] By 1929, there were 55,000 domestic LPG customers in the United States, and distribution of the fuel had been extended to all states.[6] Besides home and industrial use, it was used in refrigeration, flame cutting, engines and agriculture.

GASOL

TRADE MARK

Company of Dallas, adding propane and motor fuel tanks to its product lineup. Automatic Gas had been in business since 1937 and was a wholesale dealer in Automatic and Eveready gas systems. At the time of the merger, Wallace was Bender's assistant and in charge of engineering. H. Bellmire, who had years of experience working with liquid petroleum, was the plant superintendent, while H.F. Toll was in charge of the office and accounting.[31]

Wallace, who had gotten a crash course in tank building, now had to undergo his first selling trip. Bender drew him a map for a week-long excursion through San Antonio and into West Texas, provided a list of possible business contacts and sent Wallace on alone. Wallace dreaded the work at first: "I didn't know anything about selling. I'd get up to a door and always think: 'Hell, I hope they're not here so I can go home.'"[32]

But he persevered. With a mixture of gruff advice and friendly encouragement, Bender sent Wallace out again and again with the instruction "not to come back until I sold something."[33] Wallace came to view those chances to do something difficult and Bender's pep talks — some of them off-color — as great lessons.[34]

Meanwhile, Bender was looking for other products to sell and soon settled on air pump tanks for filling stations, which were added to Wallace's catalog. He took an automobile trip that

Above: A trade show promotional piece urging dealers to stop in Bender and Wallace's booth.

Left: *The Who and What*, a newsletter published by the LPG industry, welcomed Trinity Steel to the industry in its February 1947 issue. Bender, far left, was featured in an article. With him, left to right, are M.E. Rice, H. Bellmire and Ray Wallace.

took him through Ohio, Illinois and Indiana to sell some of the tanks, and he succeeded in selling several hundred.[35] Between July 1946 and June 1947, Trinity sold 4,712 tanks, the vast majority of which were for butane. The company had reached $430,440 in revenue and netted almost $41,000 in profit.[36]

This was the beginning of rapid expansion for Trinity Steel, which was prepared to benefit from swelled personal savings accounts due to overtime shifts and a lack of consumer goods available during the all-out effort to win World War II. Bender noted in a local newspaper that "the extension of modern home facilities to rural sections throughout the country has made the liquefied petroleum gas industry one of the fastest-growing industries in America. People on the farm who, a few years ago, were cooking on a wood stove now have practically all the conveniences of their city brothers."[37]

In 1948, the year Trinity Steel was legally incorporated, company sales jumped 64 percent. Its charter, granted in October 1948, stated that Trinity's mission was to "design, purchase and sell steel and iron and other metal products, and the manufacture of any or all of such products, and to design, sell, construct and erect engineering and architecture structures, and to contract for the construction and erection of structures."[38]

Above right: Trinity Steel grew out of the mule barn and moved to South Lamar Street, which was about six miles closer to the Trinity River. The river tended to flood the plant in heavy rain.

Below: Custom propane tanks at the plant on South Lamar Street.

The company was incorporated with $100,000 of stock, divided into 1,000 shares of $100 each. Bender, the largest shareholder, bought 740 shares for $74,000. Bryant, the next largest shareholder, paid $25,000 for 250 shares, and Wallace had 10 shares after paying $1,000. These three stockholders comprised the company's board of directors.[39]

On November 1, 1948, the new Trinity Steel purchased nearly all of the assets of the existing

partnership.[40] Early in the next year, Trinity Steel moved out of the mule barn and into a larger office at 3301 South Lamar Street.[41]

Trinity Steel continued to grow in the 1950s. Sales hit $1.6 million in 1951, and two years later climbed to $2 million.[42] The company added new equipment and looked for more land to expand the operation. Bender told *The Dallas Morning News* that the time had come to modernize Trinity Steel. A second automatic welding machine, for instance, "puts on a bead far superior to that done by hand. Steel-cutting operations have been more than quadrupled by the addition of a steel shear which makes a precision edge. Plans are now under way to acquire a tract of land to provide for further expansion of plant operations."[43]

Trinity Steel continued to grow. By the mid-1950s, the company was selling a variety of tanks throughout North America and Europe.

Trinity's products included storage tanks, truck tanks and transports for LPG. It also produced butane-propane tanks for domestic and industrial use, fuel tanks, and tanks for anhydrous ammonia, the liquid form of pure ammonia gas used as a fertilizer and as a refrigerating agent. By 1956, Trinity revenues passed the $3 million mark, and the company was the only manufacturer in its market to serve a wide geographical area. Its products sold all over the United States, as well as in Canada, Mexico and some European countries.[44]

Bender-Wallace Development

As Trinity grew, its leaders sought to consolidate control over their own operations. At first, the company had leased trucks from independent truck operators to deliver its completed tanks to customers. By the end of the decade, however, Wallace wanted the company to buy its own trucks to bring steel to the plant and then deliver finished tanks to customers. He and a partner, William Johnson, formed Wallace-Johnson on

July 20, 1949, to buy, lease and sell trucks, truck-tractors, semi-trailers and other vehicles.[45]

Four years later, Johnson withdrew from the partnership, and Bender and Wallace began a new partnership called Bender-Wallace in March 1953, later incorporating in 1956 as the Bender-Wallace Development Company.[46] The new corporation was involved in transportation, construction, real estate, and the sale and trade of many types of goods and merchandise. The company bought, sold and leased heavy equipment and also lent and invested money.

Trinity employed more than 150 workers in Dallas and was the world's largest manufacturer of the T-1 steel transport container, a specialized LPG container that was larger and lighter than previous models. The popular T-1 steel was a heat-treated, high-strength "trade-name" steel manufactured by U.S. Steel Corporation.

The company had also expanded its manufacturing and sales operations into Mexico. Bender and Wallace had formed a partnership with Vincente Garza Osuna, one of Trinity's largest LPG tank customers. Together they launched a company called Tanque de Acero Trinity in 1955 to build and sell tanks for the Latin American market. The venture, located just outside Mexico City, grew quickly. Within three years it had passed $1 million in sales.

Trinity Steel was a steadily growing enterprise. In 1957, it opened a 65,000-square-foot plant on a 15-acre tract of land at 4001 Irving Boulevard. The new facility had such unheard-of luxuries as air-conditioned offices, a large maintenance garage and a parking lot populated by a fleet of 23 tractor-trailer units.[47] At the facility's opening, Dallas Mayor R.L. Thornton donned a worker's apron to cut a steel ribbon with a welder's torch. Guests were taken by golf cart and tram to view the new plant.

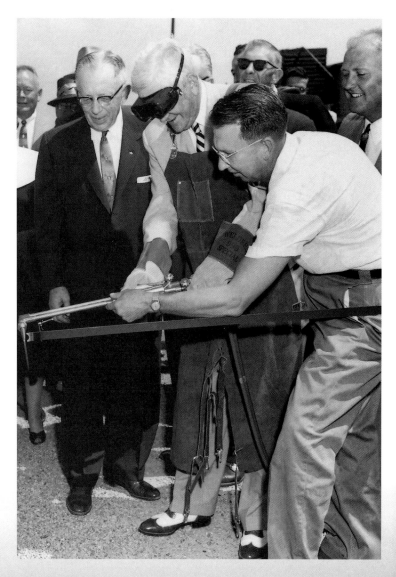

Above: Dallas Mayor R.L. Thornton, in worker's apron, cuts the ceremonial steel ribbon to open Trinity's new plant on Irving Boulevard.

Below: Ray Wallace is on the right in the group standing in front of Trinity's growing fleet of trucks.

Hidden Dangers

It appeared, however, that Bender had picked a poor time for the construction of the Irving Boulevard plant. Competitors had crowded the market just as the level of new housing had begun to fall from the frenetic pace of the early 1950s. Moreover, a glut of domestic fuel had reduced the need for new refineries, leading to a drop in the demand for storage and transportation tanks. The economic climate that had been so sunny quickly turned overcast as profit margins fell.[48]

Trinity had stretched itself too far and began to lose money. But Wallace was a survivor.

He had overcome the car accident, worked his way through college to get his degree, and helped build a prosperous business. As weaker LPG tank companies folded, Trinity Steel began negotiating with its chief competitor to join forces.[49]

Above: The Irving Boulevard plant had 65,000 square feet and featured air-conditioned offices.

Below: Trolleys took family members and guests on a tour around the facility.

The tank line at Dallas Tank in 1941. Sheets of material were draped around the line to shield the glare of welding.

CHAPTER TWO

TANKS BY BANKS

"I asked Ed Hoffman if there was any chance of the employees buy-ing this company. He said no, not if our word was any good. We made a promise to merge with Trinity Steel."

— Ed Boulter, seeking to keep Dallas Tank independent in 1958.[1]

A S COMPETITORS, TRINITY Steel and Dallas Tank knew each other well. Every day, Dallas Tank works manager Ralph Banks drove by Trinity's shiny new plant on Irving Boulevard — and every day, he felt a small pang of envy. He pri-vately believed Trinity had picked the wrong time to expand, but Banks still coveted the chance to run such a modern facility.[2]

Given the business climate, that was not likely to happen. Trinity may have stretched its resources, but Dallas Tank was floundering to the point that stockholders seriously considered liquidating the company to cut their losses. The field had become so congested it was forced to sell butane and lique-fied petroleum gas (LPG) tanks at cost.

It would have been an ignominious end to a company that was a pioneer in the area of LPG and butane tank manufacturing. Dallas Tank Company was founded in 1933 by Mack L. Vickrey, L.H. Rhea and J.F. Griffin. Begun as Dallas Tank & Welding Company, it started out in a similar way as the young upstart, Trinity Steel — in a cramped shed measuring just 16 feet by 30 feet.[3] The company first built tanks to haul and store gasoline from the refineries that dotted the rich East Texas oilfields.[4]

A year after Dallas Tank was founded, it was purchased by 37-year-old W.W. Banks, Ralph's paternal uncle. With his slogan "Tanks by Banks," W.W. Banks began to turn the little company into a thriving enterprise. By 1936, his company had earned a reputation for pro-ducing the highest quality tanks, leading W.W. Banks to sever connec-tions with his other business activi-ties to devote his full attention to his growing company.[5] Two years later, Dallas Tank was building tanks for major oil companies and building streamlined gasoline truck tanks.

W.W. Banks was born in Crowley, Texas, south of Fort Worth, on April 16, 1897. The youngest of 10 children, he and his family moved to nearby Everman, where he attended school and married Jewell Marie Chambers. He first worked for the Southwestern Mechanical Company in Fort Worth, then moved to Dallas and went to work for Wyatt Metal & Boiler Works. Over the next 13 years, Banks toiled his way up from helper to foreman.[6]

He took over Dallas Tank with one other per-son, future Dallas Tank board member Sue Gibbons. She handled the bookkeeping, a task that became daunting as the business grew. "We worked day and night because customers

William W. Banks bought Dallas Tank & Welding in 1934. He turned the company into a thriving business. *(Photo courtesy of Don Banks.)*

lined up in our office. We couldn't wait on them fast enough," Gibbons recalled in 1999.[7]

Dallas Tank & Welding entered the butane and the LPG market at the right time. Residential use of LPG was rising sharply in the United States, spurring the demand for pressure tanks. Prior to World War II, the company's efforts shifted almost entirely in this direction for several reasons. First, the fuel was extremely cheap; in fact, refineries were anxious to rid themselves of this oil byproduct for pennies rather than risk flaring the combustible material. Second, customers living in rural areas beyond the reach of gas mains recognized butane and LPG as cheaper, healthier, safer and more convenient than wood or fuel oil.

Though the rest of the country was mired in the Great Depression when Dallas Tank was founded, Texas (and East Texas particularly) was booming. Only three years before, the only known supergiant oilfield in the continental United States was discovered in East Texas, and any business related to the oil and fuel industry profited handsomely. W.W. Banks was deservedly proud of his company's role in Texas' highly profitable oil industry. Along with butane-propane systems and equipment, Dallas Tank built smoke stacks and steel plate fabricators. In 1939, Dallas Tank recorded $234,000 in sales.[8]

Dallas Tank was one of 10 oil-well supply companies, including equipment makers and suppliers, listed under a two-page *Dallas* magazine advertisement in early 1940 that proclaimed, "Oil Well Supplies ... Keep Many Wheels Turning." *Dallas* magazine went on to note that Dallas had 289 supply companies and that such companies fed employees, as well as the oil industry.

Above: Sue Gibbons handled bookkeeping for Dallas Tank and eventually became its secretary-treasurer when the company was incorporated. *(Photo courtesy of Sue Gibbons.)*

Inset: Workers pose for this 1941 photo. *(Photo courtesy of Don Banks.)*

Below: Dallas Tank, shown here in 1940, was incorporated in 1939. *(Photo courtesy of Don Banks.)*

"Many Dallasites think of oil well supplies as necessities for the development and maintenance of Texas' great oilfields. Oil well supplies sold in Dallas not only help to keep these wheels turning but contribute greatly to the economic and civil progress of this city. Two hundred eighty-nine firms engaged in supplying the oil industry maintain or contribute to the support of more than 10,000 Dallas citizens."[9]

After the United States' entry into World War II, Dallas Tank was one of the first in its industry to convert to wartime production. Workers produced torpedo tubes for destroyers and submarines, air-receiving and hot-water storage tanks for the Army, and buoys, floats, gasoline skid tanks, bomb-shipping rings and hatch covers.[10] Dallas Tank was also a major producer of pontoons, or floating bridges. These pontoons enabled military forces to cross rivers where bridges were either nonexistent or destroyed. Banks himself was a member of the War Labor Board for the Dallas area.[11]

In 1942, Banks' 18-year-old nephew, Ralph, joined Dallas Tank as a 30-cent-an-hour helper. Ralph Banks had grown up on the family farm in Denton County, north of Dallas.[12] Like Ray Wallace, Ralph possessed a strong work ethic. "I

never had anything to offer the company except hard work," he noted in 1998.[13]

Two months after he started working for his uncle, Ralph Banks enlisted in the Navy, serving most of his 34 months in Africa and Italy. During leave, he married Marjorie Pollard, a coworker at Dallas Tank: "She tells everyone that she's got seniority on me," he later liked to joke.[14] After the war, Ralph became a trainee in an air-conditioning company. But Harry Leyda, the company's executive vice president, told Marjorie Banks, "I have a job here for him. We want him back." Ralph asked Leyda why because Ralph hadn't been there very long. Leyda responded, "Every man in that shop claims that you were the best worker they ever had."[15]

In the time Ralph Banks was gone, his uncle had shortened the company's name to Dallas Tank. Among the reasons given, W.W. Banks felt that "'& Welding' in the company name tends to cheapen the style of the corporation and that many persons gain the impression that the company is comparable to some backyard welding repair shop."[16]

Among its other wartime products, Dallas Tank built pontoon bridges using scrap metal collected by civilians during World War II. *(Photo courtesy of Don Banks.)*

so brisk that "at times it was hard to get enough steel to do everything we wanted to do."[20]

Dallas Tank was also recognized as a leader in the community. The company sponsored bowling teams, which participated in Dallas leagues, and W.W. Banks himself became involved in other businesses, such as the Trinity Oxygen Company (no connection with Trinity Steel) in Fort Worth, and was a director of the Oak Cliff Bank & Trust Company in Dallas.[21]

The same year the book went on the market, *Dallas* magazine published an article called "Home Industry." It reported on the various locally owned firms in Dallas County, noting that the area had 1,507 manufacturing

After the war, Dallas Tank returned to the LPG tank business and added anhydrous ammonia storage and transport equipment, as well as refinery equipment, to its product lines.[17] Like Trinity, Dallas Tank expanded quickly, and W.W. Banks was honored in the Dallas business community. A 1948 book titled *Texas Edition of Men of Achievement* lauded the businessman: "There is a popular saying that nothing takes the place of experience. In the life story of William Walter Banks there could be no truer statement."[18]

The book noted how Dallas Tank had mushroomed from a $2,000 firm to one worth more than $400,000, from two employees to about 200.[19] The history of Dallas Tank was a "typical American industrial romance," and "continuous growth on a sound foundation, fortified by the experience and driving power of President Banks, has established the Dallas Tank Company, Inc., as a leader in the welded sheet and steel plate fabricating industry. 'Tanks by Banks' is a slogan with a meaning." John Banks, Ralph's brother, recalled that business was

Above: Believing that the "& Welding" portion of the name cheapened its image, W.W. Banks shortened the company's name to just Dallas Tank. *(Photo courtesy of Don Banks.)*

Right: This 1946 advertisement celebrated Dallas Tank's rapid growth under Banks' ownership. *(Photo courtesy of Don Banks.)*

Growing . . .
WITH THE SOUTHWEST

In 1934

Starting business in 1934 with two employees and one 14 x 30-foot building on a 50 x 100-foot lot was the small beginning of the Dallas Tank Company, Inc., twelve years ago.

In 1946 — A 4½ Acre Plant — 200 Employees

From 420 square feet of floor space to 40,000 square feet of floor space . . . from two employees to two hundred . . . all in the space of twelve busy, crowded years is the story, briefly told, of growing with Dallas. Today Dallas Tank Company, Inc., does a national business from coast to coast and border to border fabricating all types of welded sheet and steel plate products.

201-5 WEST COMMERCE STREET   •   P. O. BOX 5387   •   DALLAS, TEXAS

plants, at least 80 percent of which were "home-owned."[22] The article painted a flattering portrait of Dallas Tank:

"One Dallas home industry could easily have been used to give a miniature sketch of all Dallas industry, for it is typical in every detail. Dallas Tank Company is a young company, enjoys an international trade, and is the result of one man's business genius which has parlayed a $2,000 investment into a firm which has over $2 million volume of sales annually. 'Tanks by Banks' is a slogan that has become well known throughout the Western hemisphere during the 15 years that W.W. Banks has been building tanks in Dallas."[23]

Stumbling Toward the Edge

Dallas Tank headed into the 1950s a strong company that basked in its own prosperity. In January 1953, Dallas Tank went public. At the first annual stockholders' meeting, held on September 27, John Rauscher of Rauscher, Pierce & Company, which underwrote the offering, reported that people throughout the state were rushing to buy the stock. "I think that is a fine thing for the company and a fine thing for the stockholders that was done," Rauscher said. "We have confidence in the company."[24]

At the same time, the board of directors was enlarged to nine directors, including W.W. Banks;

Sue Gibbons; Meyer Rachofsky of Mercantile Bank; company counsel Alto Cervin; E.O. Haltom, Dallas Tank's general sales manager; Malcolm Reed, executive vice president; T.J. Tennison, Jr.; W.W.'s nephew, John W. Banks, vice president; and John Rauscher.

At that first board meeting, the board made a decision it would later deeply regret: the majority purchase of the Vicksburg Tank Company in Vicksburg, Mississippi. Vicksburg Tank was losing money at the time, but W.W. Banks was convinced that his company could make it work, and he believed the locale would lower shipping costs. "Vicksburg can ship tanks into St. Louis by barge lots with about 10 cents to the dollar of what our freight would be out of Dallas," Banks noted.[25] Vicksburg Tank later merged with Dallas Tank, and the company letterhead referred to the Mississippi operations as the "Vicksburg Division." C.C. Caloway Jr., vice president of Vicksburg Tank, joined the board of Dallas Tank.

The hope of using the Vicksburg plant to ship product economically was soon dashed. In 1954, the new division of Dallas Tank lost more than $9,600 on sales of $350,000.[26] Much of this loss

Dallas Tank Company was known synonymously by the moniker "Tanks by Banks."

BROTHER BILL HARROD

WILLIAM LEO HARROD WAS A tough-talking and ham-fisted welding foreman for Dallas Tank & Welding. It was said that he was once a drinking partner of the infamous bank-robbing team of Bonnie Parker and Clyde Barrow and was himself famous for his fighting prowess.

But it was the strength of his beliefs and his compassion for which he would be remembered. Harrod got religion. He became an ordained minister, a self-described preacher of a "real hellfire sermon," and it wasn't long until Brother Bill became known nationally for his work with the poor.[1]

Harrod kept his $80-a-week job at Dallas Tank after he became a minister because his congregation could only pay him $10 a week, and he still had a family to feed. But he came to a life-changing decision on one wet and cold December day in 1943. He saw his congregants, most of whom worked outdoors as laborers, suffering from the cold weather because they lacked proper clothing. Children often

missed school because they had no shoes. Harrod asked himself a question: What was more important to him, people or his work?[2]

A newspaper article gave this account of what happened after Harrod's soul-searching: "He went up to the Dallas Tank [&] Welding Company Superintendent Brummit and said, 'Red, you can get you another welding foreman. I'm goin' to West Dallas to preach.'"[3]

Harrod and some of his 63-member congregation built a clothes closet and a food bin. He went to merchants and friends for food and clothes to give to the needy. Indeed, W.W. Banks would be noted in his obituary as helping found the Brother Bill Harrod Baptist Mission. Harrod, who never advanced beyond the third grade, wanted every child in West Dallas to have the opportunity to at least finish high school. "He remembered how hard it was for him," recalled his longtime assistant Juanita Bailey, who joined Harrod in 1944.[4]

When their meager savings ran out, Harrod and his family ate from the church's food bin and wore clothes from its clothes closet. But his congregation grew, and his annual shoe-giving parties became famous. He also returned regularly to his old job site, a 1950 article noted. "Every second Wednesday noon, Bill Banks gives his men 30 minutes off and Harrod preaches at the very Dallas Tank [&] Welding Company he quit seven years ago."[5]

Banks had promised to pay his workers regular pay during the evangelistic services and, in the early 1950s, he gave Harrod $1,000 to buy land for a camp for West Dallas boys and girls. This eventually became the mission on Palacios Avenue, which was renamed the Bill Harrod Memorial Baptist Mission. Brother Bill retired reluctantly in 1969, but he had a strong cadre of people to continue the work. He passed away in 1976, at the age of 72.

was caused by excessively high transportation costs at the Vicksburg plant. It turned out the plant did not have railway access and was not next to the Mississippi River. Even using trucks was hazardous because much of the plant was located near a cliff.[27]

Things weren't going so well back at Dallas Tank either. In 1953, the company was hit with a labor strike that lasted for six months. As workers picketed the plant, some large-volume orders were canceled.[28] But by January 1954, W.W. Banks was able to report to stockholders that production was back to normal, employees were no longer represented by the labor union and Dallas Tank had a backlog of orders of about $850,000.[29]

"The union dissipated because we fought it," said Ralph Banks. "Some of the employees came back to work.... They walked the picket line six months, but that's the only union we've ever really had."[30]

Although sales fell by $200,000 in 1954, down to $2.3 million, net income only dropped by $15,000, down to $113,600.[31] The financial performance was manageable considering the confluence of bad circumstances.

Then tragedy struck. W.W. Banks' wife, Jewell, died on July 17, 1955, at the age of 55. She had served as a director from 1934 to 1952 and also as a vice president during most of that time. The board recorded its sorrow at her death and described her as one "who was esteemed by her associates, loved by her friends and respected by all."[32] Then in 1957, the market for LPG collapsed, and W.W. Banks recommended to the board that the company should sell the Dallas plant and move to Vicksburg, where he believed labor rates were lower.[33] Nothing came of the suggestion.

Under New Management

Although the move didn't happen, it represented a shift in W.W. Banks' attitude toward his business: He wanted to sell his interest in the company and step aside. When this knowledge became public, two local groups vied to buy controlling interest.[34] In August 1957, he resigned, and Samuel B. Ballen, one of the inter-

Charles Sammons was the embodiment of the classic American "rags to riches" story. It was Sammons who encouraged the eventual union of Dallas Tank and Trinity Steel. *(Photo courtesy of Baylor Media Services.)*

ested bidders, replaced him as president and chairman of the board.

Although Ballen and his partners, Jerome Crossman and Edmund Hoffman, held the largest interest, their position was perhaps overshadowed by the legendary Charles Sammons, who held the largest minority share. A major player in the Dallas economy, Sammons has been described as one of the leading entrepreneurial spirits in Texas business history. He was worth an estimated $1.3 billion when he died in 1988 at the age of 90.[35] "He moved with a flair in his own operations," remembered Jess Hay, who replaced Sue Gibbons as Dallas Tank's corporate secretary.[36]

When Sammons moved into Dallas Tank, the LPG container industry was in trouble. The market for the tanks collapsed in 1957, driving both

Trinity and Dallas Tank into the red. Sammons, who held stakes in both companies, knew something had to be done. Dallas Tank was losing between $2,000 and $4,000 a month on the Vicksburg plant alone, with no end in sight to the bleeding.[37]

W.W. Banks was no longer a guiding hand for Dallas Tank — although at age 62, he was not yet ready to retire. In January 1958, he paid $94,000 for the Vicksburg operation, resigned from the board of Dallas Tank and headed to Mississippi with his nephew John to try his hand at a new tank manufacturing venture.

Following Banks' departure, the company's management changed with alarming regularity; over a one-year period, four presidents or acting presidents controlled the company. In October 1957, Samuel Ballen, who was chairman and president, ceded the presidency to Ed Ponkey, who had been hired two months earlier as general manager. Six months later, with morale plummeting and losses mounting, Ballen fired Ponkey and

John Banks, nephew of W.W. Banks, at a trade show. The climate for the tank business turned stormy as competitors crowded the market in the late fifties. John left Dallas Tank with Banks.

his executive team and turned to Harry Leyda, the former company executive who had hired Ralph Banks. Leyda died five months later. The company mourned the death of its "beloved president," and in a board resolution lauded "his devotion and immeasurable contributions to the Company.... Harry L. Leyda's abiding dedication to the highest principles in his business life and in his associations with people everywhere has served as an inspiration to us all. He was loved by all the employees of the Company."[38]

Ed Boulter, administrative assistant to the president, became acting general manager and de facto president until a new president was found. Meanwhile, he plugged the financial holes as best he could. His task was made more complicated because members of Dallas Tank's engineering department had recently left the company.

Ballen was justifiably worried about Dallas Tank's future. At a special meeting of the board in September 1958, he recommended that the company "be liquidated, the reason being that he did not believe that it could be rehabilitated in its current condition and that he did not believe that a satisfactory merger or combination could be negotiated with one or more of the Company's competitors."[39]

Most of the board resisted the idea. Sammons in particular, with large investments in both Trinity and Dallas Tank, believed that combining the talents of both companies was the best course. Boulter was hesitant to let Dallas Tank's independence go, and he explored the possibility of the workers buying the company if they could raise the capital. By then, however, a deal had been struck with Trinity Steel.

At a special meeting on the morning of October 29, 1958, Dallas Tank shareholders overwhelmingly approved a merger with Trinity Steel and Bender-Wallace Development for 188,453 shares of stock.[40] Dallas Tank shareholders also approved changing the name of the corporation from Dallas Tank to Trinity Steel Company, Inc. A new company had been born.

The yard at the Irving Boulevard facility. The first order of business was to consolidate manufacturing at the plant.

CHAPTER THREE

WELDED TOGETHER

"That's how we built Trinity, by showing confidence in our workers. We gave them the things they needed and made sure I was around on the floor to help. If I worked 11 hours a day, I was on that floor for seven or eight of them. The people knew I was there to help them, and in turn, they all wanted to help me and the company."

— Ralph Banks, 1998[1]

SOON AFTER THE MERGER between Trinity and Dallas Tank, the normally media-shy Charlie Sammons revealed the secret to his success during a rare interview with *The Dallas Morning News*. The self-effacing Sammons said he possessed "no particular skill and no college training" but instead relied on finding and encouraging the right people to work for him.[2]

This was a key element in his plan for Trinity. Sammons and the other board members had already recognized the potential of the energetic W. Ray Wallace, even though the 35-year-old had never been tested as president of a publicly owned company. Shortly after the merger, his uncle, C.J. Bender, was named chairman of the board to provide advice and guidance, while Sammons stayed in the background, giving encouragement and asking the ever-important question, "But Ray, will you make any money?"

The merger was completed on November 1, 1958, and Wallace began the first day of a 40-year odyssey as the leader of Trinity. His first order of business was to consolidate manufacturing in the Irving Boulevard plant. The Dallas Tank plant was put up for sale, and the company began to rationalize its workforce between the 200 to 250 employees at Dallas Tank and the 150 workers at Trinity. Wallace also put a long-time Trinity employee in charge of the plant. Ralph Banks, meanwhile, went to work with customers to process and schedule work orders.

Despite the sunny expectations of local business periodicals, like *Dallas* magazine, which predicted that the combination would boost productivity and quality, Trinity continued to suffer under a flow of red ink. The company reported a loss of $347,000 on almost $4 million in combined sales for 1958.

"Favorable operating results were not achieved," said Bender. "Part of the loss consisted of charge-offs to bring inventories and accounts receivable down to realistic bases." He said he appreciated the "sustained and loyal efforts of our employees during the trying period in which we have been engaged."[3]

Good will didn't pay the bills, however. Wallace held meetings every Saturday morning to discuss ways to straighten out the tangled lines of production, control inventory and establish lines of authority. Dick Martin was a regular attendee of these weekend sessions. Martin had started with

---

W. Ray Wallace was named president of Trinity Steel. His uncle, C.J. Bender, became chairman.

Dallas Tank in August 1957, moving from the Texas oilfields to work as an engineer.

"He was totally in touch with everything that was going on," Martin remembered. "When he talked to you about improving a process, he wanted to know everything about that process."[4]

Wallace was described by those who worked with him as a leader blessed with the ability to listen to his employees and take suggestions. Edmund Hoffman, a longtime board member, described Wallace as honest, decent and friendly.

"If he needed to be tough, he'd be tough, but he was always fair and always honest. And trying to figure out what to do and how to do it, and what can we now make that we weren't able to make two years ago.... Ray and the employees kept working. That's all there is to it because otherwise, you can't grow."[5]

"Mr. Manufacturing"

Even after consolidating operations in the Irving Boulevard plant the company was still losing money. "Morale was poor, quality was disastrous and efficiency was deplorable," said Ralph Banks.[6]

Finally, in May 1959, Wallace called Banks into the office and said, "Ralph, I need you to go down and take over the plant. We're losing $35,000 a month since the merger. We didn't have that kind of money to lose in the first place."[7]

Above: Dick Martin started at Dallas Tank in 1957. He would eventually rise to become vice president of Trinity Industries.

Right: Ralph Banks, nephew to Dallas Tank founder W.W. Banks, was told he would have "two or three" opportunities following the merger.

This was exactly the opportunity Banks had hoped for but didn't expect in the days when he would drive by the Trinity plant — and it was one that Wallace had hinted at. During the merger, Wallace had toured Dallas Tank and was impressed with the way Banks ran his shop. "Your security with the company is good," he told Banks. "We will have two to three specific opportunities."[8]

Seven months later, with the plant steadily losing money, Wallace asked Banks to untangle the mess. "I asked him 15 questions about the situation," Banks recalled. "He answered 14 of them. The last question was 'How soon do you expect to see improvement?'"[9] Wallace left the question unanswered, only saying, "I want you to take and run it as if you own it."[10]

In fact, ownership was at the very heart of the plant's troubles. So many rapid changes had occurred with the merger that the plant's workers were left bewildered and anxious. They didn't know who was running the plant and who would remain. Yet Banks had a deep, abiding faith in the work ethic of the individual and now had the authority to reorganize the plant.

"There are a lot of people in this old world who think people don't want to work," said Banks in a 1998 interview.

"I don't believe that. If you give people basically three things: the right tools, the right material and reasonably correct instructions, they'll work. That's how we built Trinity, by showing confidence in our workers. We gave them the things they needed and made sure I was around on the floor to help. If I worked 11 hours a day, I was on that floor for seven or eight of them. The people knew I was there to help them, and in turn, they all wanted to help me and the company."[11]

It only took a month to turn it around. A pleased Wallace later called Banks back into his office. "He remembered my 15th ques-

Trinity's new management applied a firm yet fair hand to the workers. The plant was soon making money.

tion, which at the time he didn't answer. But now he said, 'I'm going to tell you: 30 days. Not only did you turn it around, you made money.'"[12]

Banks' ability to sort through a manufacturing nightmare, fix snarls and motivate the workers became legendary. He would soon be known as "Mr. Manufacturing," and his input on future acquisitions would be crucial to Trinity's success.

Jess Hay, corporate secretary and attorney for Locke, Locke & Purnell, said that despite the initial problems, the merger was successful on two levels. "One, it strengthened the combined company financially. It broadened the revenue base. Two, it gave Ray more to work with as he launched his own career as CEO. I think it was a very, very fortuitous marriage for investors, and it was great as a launching pad for the second stage of Ray's career."[13]

The company was reborn at a propitious time. Prodded by President Dwight Eisenhower, Congress had passed the Federal Highway Act of 1956, giving birth to the modern interstate highway system. The federal government was authorized to fund 90 percent of the initial 42,500 miles of the limited-access highway, with the states making up the difference. The system was designed to allow traffic flow between the East and West coasts and Mexican and Canadian borders without traffic lights or intersections. Gentle curves, gradual grades and long sight distances would make transportation as safe as possible.[14] (The total length actually grew to 45,000 miles by the time it was formally completed in 1996, when it connected almost every major U.S. city and carried more than 20 percent of the nation's traffic.)

As work got under way on the project, it was clear that road transportation promised to bring the regions of the country closer together. In later decades, it would also provide direct opportunities for Trinity.

On the Rising Edge

Even as Banks reorganized the Dallas plant, Wallace was looking for ways to grow the company. He firmly believed that a public company survived only by growing, and the way to expand was to purchase companies with little or no earnings.

The growth of the highway system brought new opportunities to sell and ship equipment, like the refinery vessel pictured below, to customers all over the country.

What Trinity needed was a manufacturing site capable of producing LPG tanks closer to the company's larger customers. To satisfy this need, Trinity purchased a tank facility in Francesville, Indiana, in September 1959. It was the merged company's first acquisition. The plant was near customers and offered reduced freight charges for shipping to local customers.[15]

The plant was outfitted with equipment from the old Dallas Tank site on West Commerce Street, which was an expensive burden that cost Trinity $3,000 a month in taxes, utilities and depreciation.[16]

These moves still weren't enough to prevent a loss in 1960, as Trinity reported a $73,000 loss on sales of $3.8 million. A steel strike that year seriously affected supplies, making it more expensive to manufacture products, and the costly Dallas Tank plant continued to drain Trinity's coffers.[17]

In spite of all this, the future held promise, and Wallace expected that Trinity would soon be profitable again. The company had a healthy backlog of orders and was adding new products, such as new bulk commodity trailers able to handle cement, flour and chemicals.[18] By March 1960, the end of Trinity's fiscal year, Bender reported to stockholders that the company had a total backlog of more than $1 million.

On the cusp of the new decade, *Dallas* magazine featured Wallace in its "Young Men Going Places" section. The article noted that the six-foot-tall Wallace, with "keen blue eyes ... even at the young age of 36 looks every inch the executive, thanks in part to graying temples. 'Steel shortages in very recent weeks have helped this along,'" Wallace joked to the magazine writer. The article covered Trinity's beginnings and subsequent growth:

"From a small beginning, Trinity has grown into a $5 million-a-year-plus operation.... The firm produces LP gas tanks for homes and for dealer storage; tanks for LP gas delivery trucks; transportation equipment for hauling bulk dry commodities; stainless steel transport equipment for chemicals; reactors and refractionating towers and numerous pressure vessels for the oil and chemical industries; and many other items of steel. Production capacity at the 12-acre location

at 4001 Irving Boulevard is being increased, and only this year, a two-acre location was added in Francesville, Indiana. The company now employs some 150 to 200 persons."[19]

Despite the rough years behind it, Trinity entered the new decade on a high note with a new leader. Wallace had successfully managed the company's first acquisition, and confidence and morale among employees rose as bank debt fell. But, with Wallace ever eager to find new growth opportunities, the good times were just beginning.

This ad from the late fifties touted "the new Trinity story" and encouraged customers to say "Howdy to W. Ray Wallace, adopted Texan."

A Cherokee Steel worker builds a storage tank. The purchase of Cherokee Steel roughly doubled the size of Trinity.

CHAPTER FOUR

THE RISK TAKER

"I said, allow 150 hours but go for 130. The manager there thought I was lying. He said, 'Ralph, we allow 300.'"

— Ralph Banks, recalling a conversation with the manager of Cherokee Steel about production schedules.[1]

RAY WALLACE WAS NOT ALONE in his philosophy of growth through acquisition. In the 1960s, corporations rapidly diversified as they bought scores of companies. In many cases, these purchases were made merely because a particular business piqued a CEO's interest, not because the acquired company fit in with existing product lines or expertise. The prevailing theory was that good management would turn a profit, with little regard to product line.

Trinity, with the successful Francesville acquisition complete, had its appetite whetted and launched a buying spree of its own. Yet Wallace and his staff followed Charlie Sammons' advice, asking themselves the vital questions of whether the acquisition made sense and whether it made any money. Between 1961 and 1970, Trinity added 15 companies or manufacturing plants, most of which were tank manufacturers. The nontank companies were related in some tangible way, using similar materials and processes.

Sage Advice

When approaching an acquisition, Wallace looked for companies that had once shown promise but had fallen on hard times for one reason or another (usually at the fault of management).[2] With a target company in mind, he relied on the manufacturing expertise of Ralph Banks to decide if Trinity could turn the company around. "Basically, in most of the businesses that we've acquired, it was simply from the standpoint that management had wearied," said Wallace.

"When they get to doing very well, they don't want to give up any penny of the profit for the future with the shortsighted view of, 'It's all right for now.' I don't think any business can ever look at 'right now' only. You've got to be mostly concerned about right now, but you've got to always have a thought of where you're going to be three to five years down the way, and if you let competition grow, you're going to be in bad dreams."[3]

Tim Wallace, Trinity's future CEO and Ray Wallace's son, later said his father equated growth with survival. "He said the only way you're going to survive as a public company is to grow and to control your cost," Tim Wallace noted. "The way he was able to grow was to wait until there was a down cycle. Some of his business competitors couldn't withstand the cycle, and

An early Trinity logo.

Cherokee Steel built large-capacity tanks, like this one capable of storing 2,500 gallons of propane or other gas liquids.

then he could go buy them for pennies on the dollar.... Trinity grew by buying other companies at an opportune time."[4]

This strategy required a smart and patient opportunist, which Ray Wallace was, according to corporate secretary Jess Hay.

"He would wait for the right opportunity prior to moving, and he did that with greater skill and greater patience than almost any chief executive officer I've ever worked with. He was never in a big hurry but always ready to move when the right opportunity presented itself. He had a board that was generally very supportive of that type of approach to growth."[5]

The board had good reason to be supportive. Between 1961 and 1969 sales increased by a factor of 10, from $5 million to $50 million. The company kicked off this period of growth by purchasing a tank manufacturer in Lincoln, Nebraska, in 1961.

This small company added about two acres of manufacturing space.

For his third acquisition, however, Wallace set his sights on something considerably larger: Cherokee Steel in Tulsa, Oklahoma. Cherokee was as big as Trinity, and if successful, this one acquisition would double Trinity's size.

Cherokee was the ideal candidate for Wallace's approach. During an inspection of Cherokee facilities, Wallace and Banks found a large facility, about the same size as Trinity's, with equipment that was older and less efficient. Cherokee had once been successful but had sustained heavy losses since 1958.[6]

This was enough to convince Wallace, but he was reluctant to overburden Banks with more work. Banks recalled that Wallace told him, "'It's all up to you. If we bought it, I'd need you to run it,' he said. 'If you think you can run it, I think I can go to Houston and borrow the money.'

"I said, 'Well, you better go to Houston, because I can run it.'"[7]

Cherokee Steel

Cherokee Steel was originally founded as McNamar Boiler & Tank Company, a manufacturer of storage tanks and transport equipment for the liquefied petroleum gas (LPG) and anhydrous ammonia (NH_3) industries. It prospered during the early days of the industry, remembered Lee McElroy, a vice president who joined Cherokee in 1952 soon after he graduated from the University of Tulsa.

"A lot of people were just going in the business, and it was a very exciting time for the liquefied petroleum gas industry," he said.[8] Like Trinity and Dallas Tank, Cherokee Steel's customers ranged from the ordinary mom-and-pop store to the big oil and gas companies.[9] At the time,

Above: Workers at McNamar Boiler & Tank, the original name of Cherokee Steel, pause for a photograph in 1947. *(Photo courtesy of Lee McElroy.)*

Below: A farmer applies liquid fertilizer using one of Trinity's anhydrous ammonia tanks.

anhydrous ammonia was coming into wide use as a fertilizer, and McElroy doggedly pursued contacts since there were "very few records of who was in the ammonia business."

"You'd get in the town, and you'd do like you did when you went after propane business. Go to a prospect's office and see if the boss was there. If he wasn't, his employees, who could tell you were a peddler from your worn briefcase, would usually tell you that he took a slow boat to China, and you just missed the boat. But if you'd look around a little bit, he was sitting across the street drinking coffee out of the greasy spoon over there."[10]

Like Trinity and Dallas Tank, Cherokee was hit hard by the collapse of its industry in the late fifties and limped into the sixties. In September 1961, when Trinity made its bid, Cherokee had about $4 million in sales but had sustained a loss of more than $576,000 over the previous two years. These losses turned out to be an added incentive to acquire — any company that bought Cherokee would pay no taxes on its first earnings.[11]

To buy all of Cherokee Steel's outstanding stock, Trinity paid $468,500 in cash and stock. The move added 83,000 square feet to Trinity's heavy manufacturing capacity and about 200 employees at the Tulsa plant.[12]

Cherokee Steel initially became a subsidiary but later merged into the company. With Trinity's purchase, "the management and personnel of Cherokee have been retained relatively intact, although [Trinity] now performs certain accounting

Above: Lee McElroy joined Cherokee Steel in 1952 and, after the acquisition, went on to become a senior vice president of Trinity.

Left: LPG storage tanks and large refinery tanks wait for completion in the bay of Cherokee Steel.

and purchasing functions for Cherokee."[13] James Jackson was retained as president of Cherokee Steel. McElroy joined Trinity as LPG sales manager and became a vice president in 1964. He would work for Trinity for the next 35 years, retiring as vice president.

As the deal neared completion, Trinity leaders were looking forward to ramping up production at the Cherokee operation — a task that shouldn't have been too challenging considering Cherokee's relatively low production. Just before the acquisition was complete, Banks toured the facility and found out the company needed 300 hours to build a 30,000-gallon tank. He and Wallace were floored.

"The plant manager asked me how long we took to build the same size tank," remembered Banks. "I said allow 150 hours but go for 130. The manager there thought I was lying. He said, 'Ralph, we allow 300.'"[14]

Banks worked seven days a week for six months to get the plant running up to Trinity's standards. Cherokee's basic problem was that its previous owners neglected to reinvest in the plant. The equipment was old and its organization poor.

Under new management, however, Cherokee Steel became the key to Trinity's rapid growth in the 1960s.[15] Board member Edmund Hoffman said the addition of the Oklahoma plant was necessary for Trinity to expand its product lines. "With the location and a sales force and a manufacturing facility, we were able to start building market share," he said.[16]

With Cherokee Steel revitalized, Trinity began selling oil wellhead equipment to Oklahoma's drilling companies, which thrived in the state's oilfields.[17] It also produced oil and gas separators, heat treaters, and storage tanks and distributed drilling fluids or muds, casing, tubing, blowout preventers and pressure gauges.

Oil and gas companies were particularly anxious to snap up natural gas storage tanks

---

Completed Cherokee tanks are readied for delivery in the Tulsa, Oklahoma, yard. Inefficient and lumbering prior to Trinity's purchase, the Cherokee plant was quickly "Trinitized" and soon showed a profit.

because of spot shortages that were occurring throughout the country. By the end of 1962, Trinity's sales had ballooned by 92 percent compared to the previous year, with revenue reaching $10 million and profits of more than $248,000.

Trinity's stockholders had a machine to thank, in part, for the impressive performance. A German-made welding machine reduced the man-hours necessary to built a large storage tank by more than half, explained Dick Martin. "It actually put the vessels together.

"One man could roll the rings of steel where you usually needed three people. It welded the inside and the outside manually or semiautomatically. It really cut out the labor totally of the storage tank.... [As of 1998] it is still operating over at Plant 22 in Fort Worth. That machine really captured the market."[18]

From Signs to Beer

Wallace insisted that flexibility was one of the keys to survival and success. The semi-automated rolling process led Wallace to create a Specialty Products Department in 1962 with the strategy that if one business segment fell off, as the tank business clearly had several years earlier, the company could shift to another more lucrative product line. Trinity added new steel-related products quickly. The purchase of a plant in Denton, Texas, put Trinity into the steel pole market. The poles were used for lights in the thousands of shopping malls that were springing up all over the United States and supported the display signs that would soon become a familiar presence along the expanding highway and road systems.

Trinity also became one of the country's biggest suppliers of brewery vessels, supplying fermentation and storage tanks to such beer behemoths as Miller Brewing. In the late sixties, the beer industry was nearing the end of regional battles between brands. In the next decade, breweries fought on a national scale for the hearts and thirsts of beer drinkers, especially following the purchase of Miller by Philip Morris.[19]

This movement toward national brands spurred the demand for larger and more efficient

vessels. After installing a number of Trinity's tanks, brewers asked the company to add a level flange on the top of the vessels, to which they mounted a motor that was attached to an impeller to keep the brew in suspension. The key to the contraption was a filter that strained the solids out of the brew so workers could bottle beer right from the tank rather than purify the beer by passing it through a cumbersome network of pipes.

Trinity quickly became one of the nation's leading tank suppliers to the beer industry, and

A 1,500-ton press used to make tank ends at Cherokee Steel in the late 1950s.

the specialty products line grew in importance, quickly edging out sales in the unpredictable oil-drilling market. In 1961, for instance, sales to that industry ran about 20 percent of total revenues; three years later they had fallen to just 3 percent. By 1965, the percentage would make up a paltry 1.5 percent of total revenue.[20]

Trinity's most important products, however, remained liquefied petroleum and anhydrous ammonia, which accounted for 79 percent of sales in 1965. One of the three largest builders of tanks and transports for LPG and anhydrous ammonia in the country, Trinity's market share amounted to almost a quarter of the entire market — more than 22 percent.[21] Its products included transport equipment ranging from 1,200 gallons to 12,000 gallons that were mounted on trucks, trailer frames or barges. Bulk storage tanks could hold from 2,000 gallons to 60,000 gallons, and domestic storage tanks had capacities ranging from 100 gallons to 1,000 gallons of LPG or anhydrous ammonia.

Trinity's production of anhydrous ammonia tanks gave it an unexpected footnote in a Texas-size scandal. According to one account, Trinity, as "one of the country's foremost producers of anhydrous ammonia containers in the early 1960s ... did a great deal of business with a certain West Texas promoter named Billy Sol Estes.

And Trinity was one of the few companies that managed to collect all the money it was owed by Estes before his paper 'empire' — financed by mortgages on anhydrous ammonia containers, most of which did not exist — collapsed and set off a national uproar in 1962."[22] Estes was convicted of a multimillion-dollar swindle involving nonexistent fertilizer tanks backed by federal agriculture loans and was sentenced to federal prison.

Room to Grow

The company was still exposed because most of its revenues came from just a few products. A downturn in those markets could have had serious consequences for the company and its workers.

Fortunately for the company, times were still good in the tank market. In 1964, Trinity was thriving, with sales reaching $15 million and profits of $624,000. That summer, the company began paying quarterly dividends to stockholders. Bender told directors at a June meeting that Trinity's "operations during the four fiscal years ended March 31, 1964, had been such that in his judgment and in the judgment of the President of the Company, the Board of Directors should consider establishing a quarterly dividend policy with respect to the Company's common stock and

A Trinity-built LPG tank with a capacity of more than 10,500 gallons. In spite of efforts to diversify, LPG and anhydrous ammonia accounted for almost 80 percent of the company's revenue.

Oil and natural gas companies were eager to buy refinery equipment, pictured above in different stages of production.

that, in the judgment of the management of the Company, an appropriate quarterly dividend would be 12 cents per share."[23]

That amount, paid on July 31, 1964, was the "first quarterly cash dividend the company has declared in a number of years, as it has been plowing earnings back in expansion moves."[24]

Trinity also boosted its presence in Mexico. In 1964, the company negotiated a 49 percent interest in a company called Cabezas de Acero Kikapoo, with the majority of stock held by a Mexican steel operation called Altos Hornos de Mexico. Altos Hornos had been run by an American entrepreneur named Hal Pappy. Toward the end of World War II, Pappy saw huge potential in Mexico and launched several steel concerns in Monclova, in the northeast region of Mexico, about 100 miles from the

Rio Grande. He gradually sold pieces of the company to the Mexican government, which eventually became the largest shareholder, though he remained in charge of the enterprise. Monclova is today one of Mexico's largest centers of steelmaking.

The mill had been supplying a substantial amount of steel plate to Trinity when Pappy approached Wallace. In return for price concessions on finished tanks, Trinity received a "decidedly more competitive cost position," recalled Wallace. The price was a welcome advantage but not the most important one, he explained.

"The principal advantage was that we had a very modern process to make the tank ends compared to what we had in Tulsa. So we had a lower cost product that was of better quality as far as Trinity was concerned. It was a cold-form process, which afforded closer tolerances as far as circumference was concerned. We had been using a hot-form process, which is less forgiving."[25]

This was the second partnership that Wallace had forged in Mexico. He was already working with the Mexican-operated Tanques de Acero Trinity, S.A. (TATSA), which had headquarters in Mexico City. (Bender and Wallace each owned about 22 percent of the capital stock of TATSA.) Both partnerships would be crucial to Trinity's future.[26]

Bender and Wallace told stockholders that the company's continually impressive performance was a "tribute to the loyalty, ability and untiring efforts of Trinity's personnel."[27] Trinity showed its

appreciation in a more tangible way when the company started its first retirement plan.

In 1965, Trinity sold 150,000 shares of common stock to pay off debt, buy additional plant equipment and prepare for a new round of acquisitions. The sale produced capital of $1.5 million, which board member Jess T. Hay said aided Trinity's growth. "It is hard to imagine $1.5 million being significant to a company," he said, adding, "It was not much money, but it was important to Trinity at the time."[28] Trinity also borrowed $1.2 million to provide for "orderly growth." In their letter to shareholders, Bender and Wallace explained that as the business expanded, its capital base had to expand as well. "We feel that these were additional steps in preparing us for the future."[29]

That future was unfolding rapidly. In 1965, with sales growing to $21.6 million and profits an impressive $759,000, Trinity prepared to take the first crucial steps in a market that it would eventually come to dominate — the railcar business.

An angle-roll machine, which formed insulation rings, stiffeners and other metal products at the Irving Boulevard plant.

CHAPTER FIVE

GROWING PAINS

"We were able to sell them on the fact that we could build their tanks for them for less money than if they did it themselves.... Not knowing better, we actually thought that was the tedious and difficult part."

— Ray Wallace, 1999[1]

TRINITY'S DOOR TO THE RAILCAR industry was opened in 1966 by Union Tank Car. An offshoot of the old Standard Oil empire, Union Tank Car was running full tilt with orders pouring in for its jumbo and "Hot Dog" cars, so named because these long tubular cars lacked the traditional high dome and underframe.[2]

The jumbo tank cars were used to transport liquefied petroleum gas (LPG) and anhydrous ammonia gas, and the Hot Dog cars served the booming chemical industry. Both types of cars gave a sorely needed competitive edge to the railroads, by then in desperate competition with the growing networks of long-haul trucking and oil pipelines.

Union Tank Car found itself falling behind its production schedule, so it took the unusual step of contracting the entire car to Trinity to complete, with an initial order of about 1,500 cars. This was the first time the company completed the entire car, which was then delivered to Union Tank Car in Chicago for the finishing touches.

Trinity won the contract because it had proven experience in producing large numbers of high-quality pressurized vessels. Trinity had been supplying just the tank portion to Richmond Tank Car for several years. "We were already in the 'round' business," explained Ralph Banks. "We were making propane tanks of all kinds,

including storage tanks, transports and truck tanks. So to build another round object wasn't a problem."[3]

From the viewpoint of the men who were responsible for the assembly, it wasn't as simple. Among his many duties during his career at Trinity, Buddy Alexander was responsible for shipping the material from Chicago to the plant in Tulsa, Oklahoma, where the manufacturing was to take place. "Union wanted us to build those cars from the rail up, using their material. But they didn't have any trucks, so I said we'd haul it. God, I think it turned out to be 300 loads," he recalled.[4] He and his team worked out the inevitable problems at night because during the day he was too busy overseeing the Tulsa operation.

Completing the whole car was Trinity's first step into the railcar industry, a watershed moment in its history. At the time, however, Wallace had no desire to get into the railcar business. After the order was filled, Trinity went back to producing just the tanks for the railcar makers, a role that the company was perfectly happy to fulfill, explained Wallace:

In 1966, Trinity Steel became Trinity Industries. An updated logo accompanied the change in name.

"We were able to sell them on the fact that we could build their tanks for them for less money than if they did it themselves. They would take the tanks and mount them on wheels and finish the car. Not knowing better, we actually thought that was the tedious and difficult part. In fact, building the tank is where the skill and expertise have to be. The rest is just assembly."[5]

Trinity Industries

Trinity continued to build just the tank portion of the cars for another 11 years and might have continued to do so if not for the actions of a major customer (see Chapter Seven).

Besides marking Trinity's first steps into the railcar business, the year 1966 was notable for other reasons. As Trinity moved into new products, its old name became more obsolete. In May 1966, as Trinity was gearing up to fill Union Tank's order, C.J. Bender explained to the directors that the time had come for a new name to reflect "the decision to implement a long-range plan of product diversification."

The name Trinity Industries was selected to show the company's present and future plans for diversification.[6] A new corporate logo of three

---

The purchase of the Hackney Iron & Steel Company, located in Enid, Oklahoma, was considered the first step toward product diversification.

triangles stacked separately to form a "T" was also adopted. It replaced the old logo of a piece of metal plate balanced by lift chains.

The $1.6 million purchase of the Hackney Iron & Steel Company of Enid, Oklahoma, prompted the name change because it marked Trinity's entry into the precision component parts market, the first step toward product diversification.

Hackney was the leading supplier of precision component parts for the chemical, petrochemical and petroleum industries. Hackney's 200 workers pressed metal heads and ends as well as tubular steel elbows and tees. It was the only sizable manufacturer of these products in the Southwestern part of the United States.[7] The purchase of Hackney put Trinity into the weld-fitting business as Hackney manufactured such items on special order using carbon steel, stainless steel, aluminum and other metal tubing or seamless pipe.

David R. Hackney founded the company after successfully selling iron in the Enid area following World War I. The company later focused on making and selling rig irons, the metal reinforcements for wooden derricks drilling for oil, because its product line tailored itself to the oil and gas industry. During World War II, Hackney Iron manufactured heavy marine equipment, such as bits, bollards or wharf posts, and sea chests. After 1947, Hackney expanded its product line to include butane and propane fittings for the growing LPG industry.

David Hackney was in his eighties when he decided to sell his plant. Lee McElroy, a Trinity vice president who helped put the deal together, recalled how much the elderly man loved his company. "The plant had these big old compressors that just boomed away all day. He liked to sit there in an easy chair and listen to the compressors and rock himself to sleep."[8]

Hackney Iron & Steel was just the first of a number of acquisitions made in 1966. In June of that year, Trinity bought Pond-Johnston, Inc., in Jacksonville, Florida. The purchase meant a new market area, as well as a new product line. Pond-Johnston manufactured small cylinders conforming to Interstate Commerce Commission regulations for the LPG and chemical industries. The tanks ranged from 5- to 120-gallon containers and meant that Trinity could now furnish a complete range of pressure vessels to the LPG industry.[9]

Two months later, in August, the Hackney Iron Division bought the operating assets of Tru-Weld Company, which had a plant in Navasota, Texas, and became a division of Hackney. Together, these two companies made weld caps to fit a wide range of pipe sizes, as well as tees, heads, elbows and return bends, pipe clamps and welding sleeves. Hackney and Tru-Weld's equipment included heat treating units, boring mills, lathes and presses up to 2,000-ton capacity. Their dies could produce more than 1,400 separate items for volume demand. Hackney and its Tru-Weld Division opened new markets for Trinity in the chemical, construction and petroleum industries and opportunities for growth in new metal processing operations.[10]

Trinity capped off that watershed year of 1966 with profits passing the $1 million mark for the first time, on revenues of $29.8 million. By themselves, the numbers showed the growth of the company. Just one year earlier, Trinity had had a net income of $759,000 on sales of $21.6 million.[11]

Several factors were behind these numbers. Where practical, the company combined its operations. Where necessary, it purchased new, more efficient machinery in those plants. In Minnesota, Trinity moved the LPG tank operations of the Northfield plant to a facility purchased in 1965 in New London; the Great Barrington, Massachusetts, plant (which was the least profitable facility) was consolidated with the plant in Rocky Mount, North Carolina; and the Francesville, Indiana, operation moved to Beardstown, Illinois.[12] The consolidations left Trinity with five LPG tank manufacturing plants, including the ones in Denton, Texas, and Lincoln, Nebraska.

The savings that resulted in reducing overhead costs were immediately invested in new, more precise machinery. The capital investment in better technology kept the production volume at the same level while cutting time and labor, which was critical because the industry was struggling with a shortage of skilled labor at this point.[13] As of early 1968, Trinity employed 950 people, an increase of about 100 from a year earlier.

Investment in equipment was never made lightly, however, because Ray Wallace and Ralph

Trinity purchased Tru-Weld, in Navasota, Texas, and made it a division of Hackney. This 1968 photo shows workers using a large cold-forming press to manufacture tank heads.

Banks kept an excruciatingly tight rein on spending. Don Hestand, a retired Trinity senior vice president, said Wallace and Banks challenged any request to make sure the equipment was really needed. If a manager wanted another forklift, it had to be because every forklift was already in full operation. "In every plant I ever managed, workers wanted more forklifts than they had," said Hestand. "They wanted to be able to just jump on one if they needed it for the moment." That did not fly with Wallace, nor did frivolous requests for trucks or company cars. Hestand recalled that Wallace questioned every request for new vehicles so thoroughly that "there was a little joke around the shop. The 'W' in W. Ray Wallace stood for 'wheels.' Mr. Wallace became vitally interested in anything with wheels."[14]

Ralph Banks was just as vigilant against unnecessary expense. Hestand remembered making a call to Banks to tell him that a shop was in dire need of a bigger air compressor. The nature of the work required a large amount of air pressure to run the machinery, and the current size was running at full tilt, but it just was not enough to keep up with production.

Banks went to the shop immediately and told Hestand that they both would stay until the shift ended and everyone cleared out. When all the workers had gone, Banks said "Okay, shut everything off. I want it quiet." They walked through the plant, and they both heard air hissing from a multitude of leaks. "Fix all those leaks and then call me, and I'll come back to talk to you about a compressor," Banks said. "But I'm not even going to talk to you about a compressor until I see you really need one." The leaks were fixed and the problem solved. Another air compressor wasn't necessary.[15]

Hestand said he learned an important lesson, one he remembered throughout his career at Trinity. "Sure, the guys were too busy to fix the leaks. But they weren't too busy to want another $30,000 to $40,000 compressor."[16]

In July 1969, Trinity purchased the Gorbett Brothers Tank Manufacturing Company of Fort Worth, along with several affiliated companies. The companies, owned by W.A. Gorbett and the canny Cleon Gorbett, manufactured pressure and non-pressure containers and heads, as well as other structural and metal products at two plants in Fort Worth and one in Abilene, Texas. One of their product lines was making truck transports for delivering gas to gasoline stations.

Don Graham worked as a plant manager in Fort Worth for Gorbett. He had grown up in the same neighborhood as the Gorbett brothers and mowed their lawns during the summer. The Trinity acquisition came as a surprise. "There was a buzz, and everyone was asking me since I was sort of a friend of the family but not a relative," he recalled. "I assured them ... they weren't going to sell it. Lo and behold."[17]

Graham was walking out of his office one day and saw several employees talking to someone he

---

Trinity purchased Gorbett Brothers in 1969. Don Graham, a future group president of Trinity's guardrail business, was a plant manager for Gorbett at the time of the acquisition.

had never seen before. "Just as I was about to tap the gentleman on the shoulder, I heard him say, 'Hi, my name is Ralph Banks, and I'm with the new owners.' That's how I found out about it."[18] The takeover process by Trinity was smooth, and Graham found that his new employers did not view acquisitions as conquered territory to be whipped.

Graham recalled that Banks toured and inspected the new plants with his customary thoroughness. "He really learned something every time he went through another fellow's plant," Graham said. "It was impossible to walk through a facility without learning something. Ralph was able to impart new ideas and innovations and extrapolate from what he saw other people do, and I think that is really what I see as Trinitized.

"I think it's a two-way street, and it always has been. If you make it a one-way street, you will very quickly find out that you don't know everything and probably don't even know enough, and I think it's always been listening as much as ... guiding, suggesting, proposing."[19]

The Gorbett purchase, obtained through an exchange of 80,000 shares of Trinity stock, added new products to Trinity's growing portfolio. With Gorbett, the company participated in the fabrication and field erection of welded steel storage reservoirs for water, oil, grain and food products. The growing urban population and increased use of water per capita seemed to create an almost limitless demand for water storage.[20] Trinity's field crews eventually installed storage facilities with a capacity for 12 million gallons of water at the Dallas–Fort Worth International Airport, which was completed in 1973.

No Market Unturned

Ray Wallace also could not stand to see any piece of equipment sit idly by as its value depreciated. He wanted it put to good, profitable use even if that meant entering entirely new markets. It was just this situation that led Trinity into guardrails, and it came about because of the tank car business. By 1969, the tank car busi-

An oil storage tank ready for shipment from Trinity's Dallas plant, circa mid-1960s.

ness was thriving. Some of the tanks were meant to carry cold-sensitive material, such as sulfur, which required the welding of heater coils to the sides of the tank. The crescent moon-shaped metal coils ran the length of the tank and were no thicker than a quarter of an inch. Initially, Trinity bought this item from a firm in Chicago. As demand for tanks increased, however, so did the price of these heater coils. "I guess they really felt they had a lock on the market because they were really socking it to us on the price," recalled Don Hestand. "We knew the price of steel, and we knew it couldn't cost too much labor to run it through the machine they used to form it. We saw right away that we needed to buy one of those machines."[21]

Trinity acquired the proper equipment and installed it in the Irving Boulevard plant. The company soon discovered that it took under 30 days to turn out all the heater coils the company needed for the year — which meant it ran about two days a month. The rest of the time, this piece of equipment went unused. Wallace often toured the plants during lunch, and not once did he see the machine run. Knowledgeable about the roll-forming process, he reasoned that it could also turn out guardrails when it wasn't forming coils.[22] The reasoning made sense; in 1966 Congress had enacted President Lyndon Johnson's Highway Safety Act that led to federal and state safety programs, including guardrail development, under the new Federal Highway Administration.

Hestand and Dick Martin worked on developing a customer base for Trinity's new guardrails, but one of Trinity's board members was skeptical about the effort. Alf Gamble, the founder of Alabama-based Gambles, Inc., had joined Trinity's board following the acquisition of his company in 1968. Before its acquisition, Gambles had been one of the largest producers of heavy bridge beams and girders in the Southeast. Alf Gamble had built up his company since its founding in 1957 as Highway Specialties Company. Gambles profited from the federal Interstate Highway project, and soon expanded into other areas of construction, supplying fabricated steel for bridges, dams, commercial buildings, defense installations and missile pad sites. In 1962, the company's name changed to Gambles, Inc.[23]

Alf Gamble had a tremendous amount of experience from his work with highway construction projects. He was not enthusiastic over the decision to enter the guardrail business, noted Hestand.

"A lot of people thought the guardrail business was a poor choice. Alf said to me one day, 'What in the world do you want to get in the guardrail business for? I work with highway contractors, and I'm telling you, it's like the rebar business. You can buy it, cut it to length, bend it to shape, and deliver it for less than the steel costs. You can't compete in the guardrail business.'"[24]

Volume is the key to success in the guardrail business. If business were good and the cost of materials were controlled, a company could make money. But Trinity was a newcomer in guardrails, and making a profit on this new product was difficult at first. "There were a lot of mistakes," Dick Martin noted.

The biggest mistake occurred as Trinity tried to fulfill its first large order to supply the guardrail for roads in Fort Worth extending from Highway 121 to Loop 820 into downtown. The sections didn't fit together because the distances between the post holes were off. The problem was discovered after the plant had produced 15 miles of guardrail.[25]

Workers piled the useless guardrail sections in the yard at the Irving Boulevard plant, three truckloads' worth stacked so high "it blocked out the sun," recalled Don Graham. Wallace couldn't stand the sight of it and finally sold it to Cleon Gorbett for about 50 cents a foot, the going rate of scrap metal.

Not long afterwards, Graham went to the dentist to get a wisdom tooth pulled. The dentist was a friend of the Gorbetts, and he didn't know Graham had gone to work for Trinity. With his fingers and instruments in Graham's mouth, the dentist cheerfully brought Graham up to date on the fate of the guardrails:

"He's drilling and pulling at my teeth, saying, 'Did you hear about old Cleon? He made an absolute killing. He bought all this scrap guardrail from Trinity and is reselling it as cattle fencing

for something like $1.50 a foot.' Cleon just turned the smooth side towards the cattle, and

it worked great. That dentist caused me all kinds of pain."[26]

Despite this ignominious beginning, the guardrail business eventually grew into a major source of revenue for Trinity. Heater coils, trailer slats and other roll-formed shapes were added to the product portfolio.

SEMCO was one of a number of acquisitions Trinity made to continue diversifying its product line. This is a boiler under construction by SEMCO workers.

A HISTORY OF RAILROADS

RAILROADS IN AMERICA HAVE HAD both a romantic and a rough history. Since the first commercial track was laid in 1828, railroads opened the North American continent to commerce and migration, linking the United States coast to coast and border to border. Interestingly, the development of the railroad in the United States had much to do with the "mislocation" of early colonial ports, such as Boston and Baltimore, two population centers that grew into thriving industrial centers. Their locations made it difficult to ship goods to the growing interior of the country because they lacked river access to the West. A flurry of canal-building, beginning in 1817, connected parts of the Midwest to the industrialized East with more than 3,000 miles of waterways. But canals were expensive to build, and they froze during winter.[1]

In the 1820s, Baltimore, then the second-largest city in the United States, began construction of the first commercial railroad from its harbor to some undetermined point. When it was finally completed in 1852, the B&O line extended all the way to Wheeling, Virginia (now West Virginia). By then,

railroads covered 30,626 miles. On the eve of the Civil War, in 1859, railroads carried more than 2 billion tons of goods, surpassing waterways for the first time.[2]

The Civil War naturally spurred railroad development but the "Golden Age of Railroads" actually began after the war ended in 1865, the year the first tank car was built. (The first tank car was built by Amos Densmore, who bolted two large wooden tubs, each with a tight-fitting cover, to a flatcar. The tank car was used to transport water to arid regions.)[3] Between 1860 and 1870 railroads grew to cover more than 53,000 miles, including the first transcontinental line. By the turn of the century, tracks spanned 200,000 miles of the country.[4]

This golden age had its practical ending in 1916, the year the federal government turned its attention to developing highways and roads. With the passage of the Interstate Highway Act in 1956, the government poured money into the highway system. Between 1958 and 1989, more than $213 billion had been invested in highways, compared to the paltry $23 billion committed to rail over the same period.[5] The new interstates were safe, modern and, above all, accessible to the average motorist. The Age of the Automobile dawned in the fifties, speeding the demise of railroad passenger service as the dominant mode of transportation.

For commercial freight, however, rail was still king. During the decade that Trinity entered the railway business, railroads carried 44.1 percent of intercity freight, compared to trucks, which carried 21.8 percent.[6]

Photo courtesy of The B&O Railroad Museum, Inc.

Besides purchasing Gambles, Trinity bought Custom Tool and Machine Company of Longview, Texas, Jackson Tank Company of Jackson, Mississippi, and Shelton Equipment and Machine Company of Amarillo, Texas. Shelton Equipment, or SEMCO, had been a subsidiary of PetroDynamics, Inc.[27]

As the decade ended, the company boasted manufacturing plants in 15 cities nationwide with a combined manufacturing capacity of more than $65 million annually. More significantly, the company had managed to diversify enough to reasonably shield itself from the economic cycles that were inherent in the tank business alone. Manufacturing for the LPG industry made up 30 percent of Trinity's revenue, followed by transportation products such as railcar containers and transports at 25 percent. Heavy construction accounted for 18 percent, while agrichemical took up 11 percent, and products for the chemical and petrochemical industries amounted to 10 percent. Tanks and other products for the brewery industry comprised the rest.[28]

Trinity could look back on a decade of acquisition, expansion and diversification. The company had grown from a mere two plants at the beginning of the sixties to 19 at the end. The diversification strategy clearly paid off when the national economy began feeling the effects of rising government deficits, unemployment and interest rates.

For Trinity, the rising feeling of malaise translated into a slight decrease in profits, from a record of $1.95 million on sales of almost $54 million in 1969 to $1.7 million on sales of $62.5 million a year later.[29] In his letter to shareholders,

Wallace noted that during the last 10 years, despite "cyclical conditions in some markets, start-up costs at new installations, acquisition costs, and a host of other problems inevitably encountered in new markets, your company propelled sales and net income ahead well over 1,000 percent."[30]

Bender and Wallace were pleased with the company's success and viewed Trinity's move into a variety of different products as crucial. In a letter to shareholders, they wrote that they were "confident about the future because we have diversified in the past."

"As recently as five years ago, most of our revenues came from sales to the liquefied petroleum gas and agrichemical industries. These two areas are very close to the company's beginnings when, over 35 years ago, it was mainly a supplier to the liquefied petroleum gas industry. Even though we expect the LPG and agrichemical areas of our business to continue to be a vigorous contributor to sales, our diversification moves have succeeded so well that such revenues now account for about 40 percent of total sales, compared to almost 80 percent five years ago."[31]

The opportunities grasped by Trinity in the sixties would bear prosperous fruit in the next decade.

SEMCO was one of 17 plants acquired by Trinity throughout the decade, a strategy which helped shield the company from the economic storm that was just ahead.

Mosher shipped more than 13,000 tons of steel to build the lower portion of New York's landmark Twin Towers.

CHAPTER SIX

PASSPORTS INTO THE UNFAMILIAR

"[Our employees'] loyalty, their eagerness, their teamwork — these qualities provide much more than just solutions to today's problems — they also spawn a justified corporate confidence, making it much easier for Trinity to chart still more diversified paths into the future."

— C.J. Bender and Ray Wallace, in a letter to stockholders, 1971[1]

IN JUST THREE DAYS, TRINITY doubled its size. With the purchase of Equitable Shipyards and Mosher Steel Company, the company's employees found themselves in uncharted waters. The acquisitions came on the heels of another achievement: the company's debut on the New York Stock Exchange. These milestones are even more impressive given the state of the economy at the time.

Since the decade of the seventies began, the national economy had been choking on a bizarre combination of inflation and recession. The combination was so unique that the term stagflation was coined to describe the malaise. The perception that American industry was in decline began to settle in as political and social commentators spoke of a "crisis of confidence."

Trinity Industries' balance sheet and production schedule told a different story.[2]

Even as the economy worsened, Trinity's strategy of economic insulation paid off with record earnings. In 1971, the year President Nixon enacted wage and price controls, the company reaped a record $2 million in profits on sales of $64 million. But Trinity's prosperous glow didn't extend to the guardrail business, where it limped along even after workers bounced back from their 15-mile-long mistake. The lag was hardly surprising because Trinity's competitors had an almost 20-year head start; they had both the know-how and the customer base. That was about to change, however, and Trinity owed thanks to the very same competitors that got it into guardrails in the first place.

Opening the Door

For more than 70 years, steel was considered a commodity of power and influence, the single most important commodity used to determine the rate of inflation — and U.S. Steel was the industry giant. When U.S. Steel set its price, other steel companies fell into line.[3]

Demand for steel had been growing steadily since the early sixties. A price war in 1968 caused a recession in the steel industry, but it was brief, and steelmakers soon enjoyed the benefits of a growing shortage. By 1973, the shortage had grown so severe that Big Steel initiated an allocation plan for its customers — in other words, rationing — based on their historic buying practices.

The purchase of Mosher Steel strengthened Trinity's girder business. With the acquisition of Equitable Shipyards just three days earlier, Trinity doubled in size.

The list price of steel more than doubled, from a dollar a foot at the beginning of 1972 to more than $2.50 a foot by the end of the year, and many of Trinity's competitors simply reneged on their contracts and forced customers to buy at the higher price. Trinity, on the other hand, remained true to its contracts, noted Don Graham, who joined Trinity in the early seventies.

"The customer was the installer of the guardrail, the one who was contractually obligated to a state agency to keep to the original bid. When our competitors tried to get them to buy at the higher, more current price, they went looking for someone else. Where did they look? To that old sleeping dog down in Texas, Trinity. Suddenly, we were selling beyond just Texas and Oklahoma. We sold in the backyards of the big guys, in North Carolina, California, Florida, Connecticut, Ohio...."[4]

Graham had two thoughts at the time: "One, that was really stupid of them to let us in the door like that. Two, now that we're in the door, we had all these new relationships nationwide."

The relationships Ray Wallace maintained with customers and suppliers were one of the underpinnings to Trinity's success. Wallace knew where the line lay between being cost conscious and being exploitative of a relationship. "He was always very clear that he would not do anything unethical, like revealing a competitor's price," commented Reuben

Perin, a retired vice president of U.S. Steel. "You gain a lot of respect for someone like that."[5]

Perin recalled that at one point U.S. Steel could not supply steel at the right price to Trinity. This was especially frustrating for Perin because he had worked particularly hard to establish Trinity as a major customer. The company had eventually grown to become one of the steel company's biggest buyers. But when it came to delivering the hot-rolled sheets used in guardrails, U.S. Steel was stuck.

"We ran into pricing problems to the point where the product was no longer profitable. Ray was understanding but he was cost-conscious; he wasn't going to pay a premium. He asked me, 'Are you sure?' We just couldn't file down the price anymore. He turned to several people in the room and said 'Well, maybe U.S. Steel should just not be considered for this product. That will not be held against us or against U.S. Steel. The economics are so far away from what they can afford that we just won't consider them until Rube here comes back and says they want to be considered again.'"[6]

It was a very realistic approach, Perin said. "Let's not drive each other nuts trying to be a supplier when we were economically out of the picture. When we could get back in the picture, we'd get an opportunity again."

Besides its guardrail business, Trinity had diversified into land development when it purchased 153 acres near the planned Dallas–Fort Worth airport, which opened in 1973. In 1970, the company had also bought almost 400 acres in Denton County, 30 miles northeast of Dallas, which stood to benefit from the new air hub.[7]

Mosher's steel went into the Texas Stadium, home of "America's Team," the Dallas Cowboys.

Trinity quickly received attractive offers for some of this acreage. Reporting to stockholders, Wallace noted that Trinity's management was "studying the possibility of developing these tracts as industrial centers, mobile home parks or other income-producing businesses."[8]

The Big Board

On June 28, 1972, Trinity's stock began trading on the New York Stock Exchange (NYSE) under the symbol TRN in the respectable range of $12\frac{3}{4}$ to $15\frac{5}{8}$. A Dallas-based business reporter was succinct when he described the newest member of the Big Board: "Trinity is more than just another welding shop. It doesn't have any glamorous products and there's not much fascination or intrigue connected with the corporation, but it is one of the largest metal fabricators in the country."[9]

When it began trading on the NYSE, Trinity employed more than 1,800 people and had 19 plants, most in the central part of the country. In the news story that ran in the *Dallas Times-Herald*, Wallace noted that Trinity did not have any "truly 'proprietary' products, but it does have a unique accumulation of equipment and plants and expertise that puts the firm 'in a proprietary position.'

"Wallace described Trinity's position in the competitive fabricating industry as being similar to the 7-Eleven Stores in the convenience store market and Frito-Lay's chip in the snack foods industry. 'They have done a little something extra and a little bit better than their competitors to create a proprietary-type situation, enabling them to live and grow,' Wallace said."[10]

Wallace believed that its "little something extra" involved marketing approach. "We try to put enough ingredients in to give us a little better situation so that we can survive with a profit at rough times and thus give us good earnings continuity. It enables us to grow a little faster and develop faster than the ordinary welding shop."[11]

But at the core of Trinity's success lay teamwork, an intangible but very real industrial advantage that Wallace and C.J. Bender recognized and appreciated — even before Trinity made it onto the Big Board.

"We cannot stress enough how fortunate Trinity Industries is to have assembled such a group of employees. Their loyalty, their eagerness, their teamwork — these qualities provide much more than just solutions to today's problems — they also spawn a justified corporate confidence, making it much easier for Trinity to chart still more diversified paths into the future.... They have proven that talent is versatile, and that dedication, persistence and ingenuity are valid passports into the unfamiliar."[12]

It wasn't long after Trinity began trading on the NYSE that the company readied itself to add more companies to its family of steel-related businesses. Its stock went from 2.5 million to 5 million shares. In January of the following year, Wallace secured more than $54 million from a group of banks headed by Republic National Bank of Dallas.[13]

Armed with acquisition money, Trinity began looking for new opportunities. The acquisition strategy was simple: Find a steel-related business that concentrated on turning out repetitive products, send Ralph Banks through the plant to learn the operation's good and bad points, and then Trinitize the plant to achieve maximum efficiency.

Two Swift Moves

Wallace and the board of directors made their decision in November 1973, with the purchases — made within three days of each other — of Equitable Shipyards of Louisiana and the Houston-based Mosher Steel Company. The purchase of these two companies immediately doubled the size of Trinity, brought new product lines and added to current ones. The waterfront facilities on New Orleans' Industrial Canal and at Madisonville, Louisiana, permitted Trinity to fabricate larger containers and girders, which had to be transported by water. In the past, Trinity had to pass up that sort of business.

But the acquisitions brought a new set of challenges as well. This was especially true with Mosher. "The people who worked at Mosher thought they should have bought Trinity instead of the other way around," noted Jack Cunningham, senior vice president in charge of human resources. "They didn't want to accept the fact that they became part of Trinity."[14]

Longtime Mosher executive Oscar Stewart, who became president of the subsidiary, said there was a great deal of mistrust on the part of Mosher's workers toward Trinity. Most of the workers and their managers had grown up with each other; the sense of paternalism that existed was shaken when the acquisition was announced. "They had a real distrust for the Trinity family but Trinity is a good company," Stewart explained. "They treat the people they buy right," he said.[15]

Dealing with two huge acquisitions was a daunting task. Jack Cunningham spent his first year at both Equitable and Trinity, implementing new systems and procedures for payroll and bill paying — the mundane but important mechanics following any acquisition. Switching systems and procedures was one thing; integrating them culturally was quite another. Cunningham explained that Mosher and Equitable represented the extreme ends of a spectrum: "Mosher had the oxford-cloth, button-down-collar, wing-tip-shoes kind of people. Equitable, you expected all of their management to be in the Mardi Gras parade every day. So we had one group of people who were ultra-conservative and another who were a bunch of lunatics. It was kind of fun."[16]

Founded in 1921, Equitable Shipyards built barges for commercial and military uses. Below is a 200-foot hopper barge, launched in 1981.

A Brief History of Equitable

Wallace and Cecil Keeney, who had purchased Equitable Equipment Company three years earlier from its founder, jointly announced that Trinity had bought Equitable, Louisiana's second-largest shipbuilding firm and a pioneer in offshore oil and gas equipment manufacturing. The purchase was accomplished by buying the capital stock of Equity Industries, Inc., a holding company that owned all the capital stock of Equitable. The price was $3 million, plus an amount equal to net income (not to exceed $2 million) of the acquired company for the two-year period ended June 30, 1974.[17]

In the 53 years between its founding and Trinity's acquisition, Equitable built vessels ranging from innocuous, slow-moving barges to the sleek coastal patrol boats used by the U.S. Navy and Coast Guard as well as glamorous luxury yachts for the rich and famous.

A naval captain named Neville Levy, a New Orleans native, founded Equitable in 1921, when he was 29 years old. Levy had graduated in 1913 from Tulane University with a degree in mechanical and electrical engineering and then joined the Navy during World War I. Following the war, he graduated from the Navy's Submarine School in Connecticut and stayed in the Naval Reserve as he grew his barge business. In 1939, Levy acquired Equitable's Madisonville shipyard on the Tchefuncta River, producing barges for the U.S. Army and private industry.

During and following World War II, Equitable produced diesel tugs. Many were built for the military and later sold and converted into tenders to service oil-drilling rigs. (*Photo courtesy of New Orleans Public Library.*)

Levy returned to active duty following Pearl Harbor and served as submarine control commander for the Gulf of Mexico. In 1972, he would be honored as "American Patriot of the Year" by the New Orleans chapter of the Military Order of the World Wars.[18]

Meanwhile, Equitable built cargo vessels, seagoing tugboats, oil tankers, gasoline barges and icebreakers.[19] After the war, Equitable converted many of these craft into drilling tenders for the oil industry, which was rushing to meet the rising demand for fuel. The shipyard also serviced and repaired railroad tank cars, boxcars and flatcars for private operators and the government. With the increasing use of air conditioning, Equitable also designed, furnished and installed air conditioning systems and units for homes, offices and industrial plants.

In 1965, Equitable acquired Higgins Industries, a renowned New Orleans shipbuilder. Founded by Andrew Jackson Higgins, the shipyard produced the Navy's wooden-hulled high-speed patrol boats. At its height during World War II, Higgins employed more than 25,000 people, working in eight plants that turned out 1,000 boats a month.[20] Higgins Industries also produced the all-important landing craft, upon which the fate of battles often turned. A newspaper article related this story about Higgins' contribution to the Allied war effort:

"The Navy was desperate. To get fighting forces and tanks onto enemy beaches four decades ago, America needed landing craft that could roll onto the sand, drop a ramp and let the men and equipment speed off. The obvious place to turn was Higgins Industries Inc., the bustling New Orleans company that had manufactured everything from bayou racing boats to PT boats. But there was one problem: The vessels the Navy needed didn't exist. 'But we'll be glad to build 'em for you,' said Andrew Jackson Higgins, the company's hard driving founder and president. There was another problem: They had to be in Norfolk, Va., in 10 days. 'You'll get 'em,' Higgins said. Nine days later, on June 14, 1941, the rectangular vessels were finished."[21]

CHANGING AN INDUSTRY

EQUITABLE'S CONVERSION OF THE *Frank Phillips*, a 260-foot-long, 48-foot-beam vessel, played an important role in the history of offshore oil exploration because, for the first time, a crew could work and sleep on location. The *Frank Phillips* was a floating location and supply house complete with mud pits and pipe racks, equipped with stiff-leg derricks, hoisting winches, diesel generators, pumps for water and fuel transfer, a bilge system, mud pumps, and warping winches for holding the barge to the drilling platform in rough weather.[1] The tender held a crew of 38 and was used by Kerr-McGee Corporation in 1947 to bring in the first offshore oil well out of land's sight.[2]

Through the use of a tender, or auxiliary drilling barge, the platform was built smaller and at less cost. Earlier offshore structures averaged 30,000 square feet to hold the derrick and the other needed equipment and supplies, including the drilling mud. The Kerr-McGee platform, how-ever — designed and built by Houston's Brown & Root Inc. — was only about 2,700 square feet. Having all the equipment, drilling water, dry mud and chemicals on a barge meant it "could be moved from location to location, minimizing the cost of salvage in the case of a dry hole."[3]

The Kerr-McGee well itself ushered in a new age of offshore exploration. During its 37 years of operation, it would produce 1.4 million barrels of oil and 307 million cubic feet of natural gas.

In the 1960s, Equitable built the first self-propelled drilling ship, the *Glomar II*, for world-wide offshore drilling operations, followed by three more drilling ships. The 268-foot-long *Glomar II* brought in one of the first wells that opened up the oil-rich Cook Inlet in Alaska. In 1973, Equitable was honored for its contribution to the well and thus to Louisiana's offshore oil and gas industry when its owner, Cecil Keeney, was presented with a plaque in Morgan City by the 25th Offshore Anniversary committee.

Photo courtesy of Kerr-McGee.

By the war's end, Higgins had produced 29,000 of these critical vessels. And in a secret plant in eastern New Orleans, 2,500 Higgins employees were part of the process that resulted in the first atomic bombs. Using the same type of carbon found in lead pencils, workers made black graphite blocks that were hollowed out to encircle small fuel rods in the reactor where the bombs' fuel was generated.[22]

In peacetime, Higgins Industries turned to building barges, freighters and pleasure boats, but most of its activity was in repair. Andrew Jackson Higgins died in 1952 and passed into local and maritime legend for his contributions.[23]

LASH and SeaBee Barges

Equitable had $50 million in backlog orders when Trinity acquired the shipyard. With tremendous foresight, Dick Martin and Ray Wallace had researched the barge segment of the marine industry, and Trinity made the purchase at the right time. The market had been neglected for a

number of years. As a result, the existing barge fleet was old, rusting and obsolete. In addition, there was a growing need to carefully handle different types of cargo, a need that resulted in the modern concepts of "lighter-aboard-ship" (LASH) and its larger cousin, "seagoing barge carrier" (SeaBee). Both were considered a natural extension of the container revolution, and both concepts were the same: Barges filled with cargo would simply be hauled aboard the mother ship, avoiding potentially damaging cargo handlers and allowing direct shipments to factories along inland waterways.[24]

Equitable Shipyards was the first to build both type of barges, launching the first LASH in 1968 and the first SeaBee in 1970. A typical LASH barge was about 60 feet long and 30 feet wide, while a Seabee barge was about 100 feet long and 35 feet wide. Both types (called "lighters") carried cargo aboard oceangoing ships. The lighters were pre-loaded at shallow-water ports on the inland waterways of the United States and then towed along those waterways to deep-water ports. There, the lighters were loaded onto ships and taken to Europe and Asia. The SeaBee and LASH concepts never did live up to their original promise. They would eventually give way to the intermodal concept.[25]

Equitable's shipyard on the Industrial Canal in New Orleans. Tied to the dock are LASH barges.

A Brief History of Mosher

Mosher was one of Dallas' oldest companies. Purchased for $27 million, the famous steel company enabled Trinity to compete for the fabrication of multistory structural steel with expertise dating back to 1885. Mosher was founded by Theodore Mosher, a 51-year-old machinist from Peoria, Illinois, who sought a milder climate for his ailing wife, Jennie. Since Dallas was the home of his wife's brother, they had probably received glowing accounts of the growing riverfront town.[26] On March 27, 1885, at the corner of Market Street and Pacific Avenue in Dallas, Mosher rented the rear half of a 35-by-60-foot warehouse and opened the Mosher Manufacturing Company with an initial investment of about $4,000.

Above: Theo Mosher began Mosher Manufacturing in 1885, when he was 51 years old.

Below: The workforce of the Mosher Manufacturing Company, after its move to a bigger location on Lamar Street in 1890.

Though it began operation with only four employees, Mosher's reputation rapidly grew. According to one company account:

"From the first Mosher insisted on the high quality of workmanship and service which he had given his Peoria customers, and his Texas business met with the same quick success he had found in Illinois. During the first year practically all of the company's business was in steam engine repair, and by November 1885, eight employees were working standard hours: 10 hours a day, six days a week."[27]

Within a few years, the company moved to larger quarters at the corner of Ross and Carter streets, where Mosher added a foundry to provide the round cast-iron columns used for vertical support in early Texas buildings. A short time later, the company moved to a larger site on Lamar Street.

Theo Mosher died on December 11, 1893. The company was incorporated shortly after his death, and his widow became the formal head of the company while his son, William, ran the firm

from behind the scenes. William Mosher had begun working in the plant at age 11 as an apprentice, learning the business from the bottom rung of the ladder. He wasn't officially named president until 1921.[28]

At the turn of the century, Dallas was booming. The city's population increased from 10,000 in 1880 to more than 68,000 in 1900. A company history noted that "during these years Dallas was busy laying out streets for new business and residential districts, and the Mosher Manufacturing Company was busy making manhole covers and sewer grilles for these miles of streets and furnishing iron for the imposing list of new buildings being constructed."[29] Mosher also furnished the iron and steel for the old *Dallas Morning News* building, built in 1900, and supplied cast iron for the ornamental store fronts of businesses.

During the late 1920s, Mosher established itself in the field of welded steel construction. This was when the "I-beam," with a wide flange, replaced cast-iron columns as a means of vertical support. Using this new design, Mosher furnished steel for the 19-story Dallas Power & Light Company building in 1929. At the time, it was the tallest all-welded-steel building in the country.

Mosher moved its offices to Houston, where William Mosher and his brother T.J. had already established a small metal-fabricating shop, in 1936. All of its plants began operating under the name of Mosher Steel Company. During World War II, Mosher shops ran 24 hours a day to provide steel for new aviation gasoline refineries, synthetic rubber plants, chemical plants, aircraft hangars and military warehouses. As a subcontractor, the company furnished parts for ships built in Gulf Coast plants. After the war, it sent steel to South America for mining facilities and industrial developments. It organized a subsidiary based in Shreveport, Louisiana, in 1947 and later opened a plant in Lubbock, Texas, and a sales office in New York City.

Above: The all-welded skeleton of the 19-story Dallas Power & Light Company, the tallest such structure in the nation at the time.

Below: Workers weld together an I-beam, which replaced cast-iron columns.

In 1960, the year of Mosher's 75th anniversary, the company received a plaque from the American Institute of Steel Construction to commemorate its longevity as a structural steel fabricator, one of a number of awards it had received over the years. Mosher supplied the steel used in the Arch Bridge, spanning the Dallas–Fort Worth Turnpike, and won distinction when it supplied all of the structural steel for the 44-story Humble Oil Building in Houston, "one of the tallest skyscrapers west of the Mississippi River, a job that represented 20,000 tons of Mosher steel."[30] By 1970, Mosher employed 1,600 people, and its international reputation was growing rapidly. The company exported structural steel to Taiwan, China, South America, the Caribbean and the Soviet Union.

Mosher was the prime supplier of girders and beams for the 110-story World Trade Center in New York and was the only supplier of steel for Moscow's World Trade Center. In Dallas, it continued to change the shape of the city's skyline, providing the steel for the Reunion Tower Sphere and the Hyatt Regency Hotel.

Maturing

Besides doubling Trinity's sales volume, Equitable and Mosher brought another 3,600

Mosher fabricated steel for the award-winning Arch Bridge, which spans the Dallas–Fort Worth Turnpike.

employees to Trinity's payroll, which had stood at about 2,500 before the acquisitions. Now, with more than 6,000 employees, Ray Wallace decided Trinity had grown large enough to need a personnel department.

Jack Cunningham had already written the company's first employee handbook and an affirmative action program. Both worked out well, so Wallace "volunteered" Jack Cunningham to become Trinity's first personnel manager. After about a year and a half, Cunningham left Trinity for three years but returned later at Wallace's invitation. He became a vice president at age 40, one of the youngest in the company at the time, in charge of human resources.

Until Cunningham took up the post of personnel manager, those duties had been spread around, with then-CFO Ed Breeding minding the insurance and benefits for employees and individual managers doing all their own hiring.

Other changes were taking place. Prior to 1973, the standard workweek for corporate officers included Saturdays and the standard workday often lasted 12 hours. But at 5 p.m. on Fridays, Ed Breeding launched happy hour in his office. These informal affairs usually turned into brainstorming sessions, recalled Ken Lewis, whom Breeding hired in 1964. Lewis, who would succeed Breeding as CFO, said they liked to drink "Scotch and water and start talking about ways to do things better."[31]

For insurance and other reasons, Trinity did away with the happy hour, and bottles of alcohol were removed. For some reason, they wound up

in a safe in the accounting department. Shortly after he was hired by Trinity, Cunningham went to retrieve some papers from the safe. "I found it full of booze," he recalled. "The safe contained the Trinity bylaws and several good bottles of Scotch." He informed someone of his discovery, and the next time he went to the safe the alcohol had been taken away for good.[32]

The Beginning of the Railcar Boom

Following OPEC's 1974 oil embargo, demand for Trinity's most mature product — the LPG storage tank — shot up. The energy shortage had caused the "demand for large LPG containers to increase at a rate never before experienced," Wallace told stockholders.[33] LPG storage containers increasingly were being put into industrial plants, public utility facilities, hospitals and motels for daily use and as a backup in case of disruptions in the supply of primary fuels.

But the strong LPG tank demand was still a small piece of Trinity's revenue pie. By the end of the fiscal year in 1974, Trinity's overall revenue had reached $192 million, more than doubling the prior year's $95.4 million. Profits reached $5.8 million, and the company continued to enjoy a healthy mix of product lines. Structural products sales increased from 27 percent to 32 percent in that same period, and sales of marine products doubled to 16 percent.[34] In that total sales pie, containers dropped from 51 percent in 1973 to 37 percent in 1974.

At the same time, the market for containers was expanding fast to meet the need for a variety of railcar types. Several factors were behind the surge. One, the nation's tank railcar fleet was obsolete (much like the state of the barge fleet), and replacements were needed. Two, specialized hopper car containers were necessary because the plastics market was beginning to skyrocket, and buyers tended to store plastic material in the hoppers themselves rather than spend valuable time and space to unload the cars.[35] Three, the Nixon administration had agreed to sell grain at subsidized prices to the Soviet Union, which was grappling with several years of crop failures. The deal was supposed to only involve $150 million. The Soviet negotiators actually purchased more than $1 billion worth of grain — at federally subsidized prices — which ironically drove up the price of bread in the United States.[36]

Trinity thus began building hopper car containers featuring several design improvements aimed at increasing payload and shortening turnaround for shippers. They were developed primarily for transporting plastic pellets, the raw material used to make synthetic textiles, plastic containers, toys and auto parts.[37] The company was reluctant to build the entire car, however, even though demand was clearly beginning to pick up for all types of rail transport. Only when backed into a corner by one of their own customers did Wallace and his crew decide to take the plunge that would change the industry.

A jumbo grain hopper car readies for loading. These cars were in demand in the 1970s, until the Soviet grain embargo was enacted.

CHAPTER SEVEN

CRANKING OUT RAILCARS

"It was so simple, it was almost heartbreaking that we hadn't done it years before."

— Ray Wallace, explaining Trinity's easy transition to railcar production.[1]

BY 1975, C.J. BENDER HAD largely retired from playing an active role in helping to manage Trinity, but he still kept an office in the corporate headquarters in Dallas. He had overseen the growth of Trinity from a mere shed into a company that topped $217 million in revenue that year, with 25 plants in 10 states and Mexico.

The prediction Bender had made when he first hired Ray Wallace was coming true: They were building something they could both be proud of, and Wall Street was beginning to take notice. An article that appeared in *Financial World* in 1975 lauded Trinity's fiscal strength, if not its prosaic product lines.

"Until this year few investors paid attention to Trinity Industries.... But since December Trinity's stock has shot up 290 percent, taking it from a near 10-year low of 8¾ to a 10-year high of 34. Why this burst of investor enthusiasm? The answer's simple — the somewhat belated recognition of the company's outstanding profit performance in recent years."[2]

In fact, its earnings per share had risen from $1.75 in 1972 to $4.27 in 1974. The magazine noted that the acquisitions of Equitable and Mosher helped bring Trinity into the sunlight. Ed Breeding, who was the CFO, explained that the strong earnings were due in part to the specialized niches that Trinity was able to establish in its markets: tanks for liquefied petroleum gas (LPG), structural steel products for highway construction, siding for buildings, oceangoing barges and offshore oil-drilling service equipment. "Our products are heavily tied to energy, agriculture and construction," he said in the article.

"Equitable Equipment, an unprofitable marine-products builder and fabricator acquired in 1973, has turned solidly profitable.... And Breeding anticipates that marine products 'has the potential' for being the company's fastest growth area. Multi-story structural-steel producer Mosher Steel, also acquired in 1973, moved up to 'its profit potential' this year, too, says Breeding. In essence, he adds, 'We brought new life into an old-line company.'"[3]

Meanwhile, Trinity kept branching out in new directions. In 1976 it purchased the Texas Metal Fabricating Company, a supplier of heat transfer

Success hadn't ruffled C.J. Bender. The company's chairman continued to dispense advice and anecdotes from his office in Trinity's headquarters.

equipment for the energy industry. A Houston company, Texas Metal operated as a subsidiary, and its engineers designed the equipment to the thermal, mechanical and hydraulic specifications requested by customers. Unprofitable when it was first purchased, Texas Metal continued to be a source of trouble for some time. When Don Hestand took charge of the plant, he was amazed to discover the root cause; its workers and managers hated each other and in many cases were not even on speaking terms. Called on the carpet, the feuding parties were told in no uncertain terms that either they would resolve their differences or Hestand would make the necessary cuts. Before long, production schedules were developed and adhered to, costs were watched over carefully and morale was up. Texas Metal began making money after a year and a half.[4]

That year, Tim Wallace, who had spent his summers washing Trinity's trucks, graduated from Southern Methodist University with a degree in business administration. He began working full-time for Ed Boulter, vice president of purchasing, who continued the younger Wallace's education. One of Wallace's first projects was to work with a project foreman to oversee the refurbishing of 20 acres of a pockmarked parking lot at the Irving Boulevard office. The project was not a small one; the estimated cost to repair that lot was almost a quarter of a million dollars.

Over time, Tim worked throughout the entire organization, learning such lessons as labor and time standards, the art of determining how long it takes to fabricate the different products and the issues associated with each product line. Boulter noted that Wallace caught on quickly, and he reported to Ray Wallace that Tim had the advantage of liking to work with people. "He can get them to do what they need to do," Boulter said.[5] This talent was one that would prove invaluable as Tim worked in various roles throughout the company.

The Railcar Boom

By 1977, the need for all types of railcars was causing a severe shortage in the railroad industry. Boxcars and grain hopper cars were in especially great demand. Several factors were at work. A bumper wheat crop and high overseas demand led by the Soviet Union, which continued to make huge grain deals with American farmers, was by itself overloading the rail system. A strike by grain handlers in the Great Lakes area complicated matters even further because the grain was stored in hopper cars. The petrochemical industry was also clamoring for a specialized type of hopper car to haul plastic pellets — the material used to make plastic — to supply the legions of petrochemical plants that had sprung up all over the country.

Railcars had other uses besides the obvious. Federal tax laws at the time allowed individuals to use them as tax shelters. These investments were dubbed "rolling stock," and the wealthy (doctors, lawyers, investment bankers and the like) were snapping them up to lease to the railroads. The advantage was twofold. Besides the regular income generated by a lease, the owner of a railcar received an investment tax credit of 10 percent of the purchase price (which averaged about $40,000 for a single car), a direct reduction on the owner's tax bill.[6]

As the orders poured in, one of Trinity's biggest railcar customers tried to use its position to force price concessions on tanks. Terms of the deal had already been settled, and Trinity had been happily supplying just the container portion of the car. Ray Wallace traveled to the headquarters

of his customer to settle the issue fairly. After much haggling, Wallace bluntly told his counterpart that if the two companies didn't agree on a fair price, Trinity would have to finish the cars itself — in other words, become a competitor. "If you do that," Wallace recalled his counterpart as saying, "I'm going to put you out of business."[7] Wallace returned to Dallas and began building finished railcars — first tank cars and then hopper cars.

The transition from building just the container to building the entire car turned out to be surprisingly easy. "It was so simple, it was almost heartbreaking that we hadn't done it years before," Wallace said. "It was just an area that we didn't know about, but we quickly obtained some people that did know it. The engineering was far from an impossible task because Trinity had built tanks for highway use since its inception."[8]

Trinity had several advantages over its competitors. For starters, the heart of the tank car was the barrel, which put Trinity's customers-turned-competitors in a bad spot; they had to find a new source before the end of their contracts with Trinity.[9] The company also had buying power when it came to getting steel at a good price. Years of square dealing and the company's tremendous volume (made even greater with the acquisitions of Mosher and Equitable) resulted in a strong relationship with steel companies. The company's final advantage was, of course, its flexibility.

Steve Smith was a young engineer with something shy of two years at Trinity when he was called into a meeting in the Irving Boulevard plant, where Wallace was handing out responsibilities. Ed Boulter was put in charge of purchasing while Banks naturally had all of the manufacturing. Then Wallace turned to Smith and told him to get an engineering group together. Smith at the time was essentially the only Trinity engineer, or at least the only one whose responsibilities were in line with his SMU engineering degree. Ray Wallace also held an engineering degree, but he obviously had a lot more on his plate. Dick Martin, who for years headed engineering, had learned what he needed to know from his working experience, as had Ralph Banks.

Smith began the hiring process to put a staff together. In the meantime he and Martin designed a covered hopper car with a capacity of 6,130 cubic feet, aimed at increasing payload and shortening turnaround time for shippers. Developed mainly to transport plastic pellets, the hopper car could carry other dry products such as grain and resinous powders.

The design made assembly easier: The end structures could be fabricated as a subassembly and then joined to the rest of the car. With the design completed, Smith traveled to Washington, D.C., to obtain approval by the industry's governing body.

Top: Ralph Banks, or "Mr. Manufacturing," was legendary in his knowledge of the manufacturing process.

Below: One-hundred-ton gondola cars, built by Trinity and used to carry steel plates, ingots, gravel and other material.

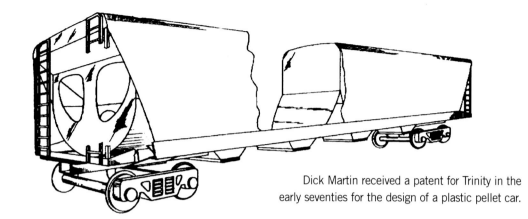

Dick Martin received a patent for Trinity in the early seventies for the design of a plastic pellet car.

Smith discovered that officers from the railroad and railcar companies held the keys to successfully competing in the industry. "It was like a fraternity, and we needed to be in that fraternity," he recalled. "We were going up against old names like Pullman Standard and Bethlehem Steel." Smith nevertheless was treated cordially. "Maybe they didn't think we were much of a threat at the time, but I created some very good friendships."[10]

This was the beginning of Trinity's involvement in the American Association of Railroads (AAR). The railroad business is somewhat self-regulating, and committees researched and made recommendations on technical issues to be decided on by the membership. The AAR was composed of competitors, but they cooperated on technical issues that improved safety and raised the bar of quality. After the usual wrangling that comes with any bureaucracy, Smith got the design approved.

But Trinity had a bigger problem than just getting a design approved. The big players like Pullman Standard and Union Tank Car had locked up supplies of components like axles and wheels. Trinity wasn't even on the map yet as a serious competitor, so suppliers were wary of committing to this upstart in the railcar market. Fortunately for the company, it had friends in the industry, friends such as the late George Green, who died in 1999. An ex-Pullman president, Green knew the right people and had the right access.

Tim Wallace was at this time in charge of putting together an inventory system to ensure Trinity had a steady supply of wheels, axles and other components to keep the railcar business

going. With a healthy order for 500 cars, Trinity got started in the hopper business. The design of the car, named the 4750 car after its cubic-foot capacity, solved an old problem. One of the most common yet expensive sections to fail was the roof because the cars twist as they travel down the track. Cracks appear near the hatch because of the stresses put upon it, much as cracks appear near doors when a house settles. Water can get in and ruin the cargo, especially in grain cars.

Racing against the clock to get the right parts by the following Monday, Dick Martin, Smith and another man, Keith Hunt, redesigned the roof, giving the structure a tubular frame. Their design was successful. Smith said that those roofs have never failed, even after 20 years.[11]

In Ray Wallace's estimation, Trinity went from building no cars in 1977 to building about 5,000 or 6,000 a year by 1980. "We really terrorized the industry. We became aware that we probably could do it quicker and easier and more economically than most of the competition."[12]

Flexing Its Muscles

Meanwhile, demand for barges was on the rise, just as Wallace and Martin expected. The net result of this activity became clear when the LPG market suddenly fell off. As one business weekly reported, "a 50 to 60 percent drop in volume in a major product line isn't exactly the kind of stuff that makes for higher profits. But the nation's largest manufacturer of LPG containers — Trinity Industries, Inc.— is producing that kind of earnings performance precisely with that experience. In fact,

Trinity is completing its fifth consecutive year of record net — one-third over the previous peak."

The secret behind the success lay in maintaining flexibility to shift from one activity to the other as opportunities presented themselves. The weekly noted that Trinity had almost entirely shielded itself from the sharp decline in its LPG tank business by increasing its emphasis on tank and hopper cars, along with heavier shipments of containers to breweries. "It has done the same in its second most important line, structural products, by stressing sales to power plants rather than highways and office buildings."[13]

After taking about a year to consolidate its gains, Trinity again purchased related companies at bargain prices with the acquisition of Delta Tank Corporation, a Georgia firm, and Houston Machinery Company, which was actually

located in Oklahoma City. Both were completed in 1977. The Oklahoma City site, bought for $1.5 million, was a 200,000-square-foot facility that included 20 acres of land.[14] In 1979, Trinity bought Heat Research Corporation, a manufacturing plant east of Longview, Texas, which gave the company the expertise to produce covered rail hopper cars.

Heat Research, interestingly enough, had been owned by Pullman Standard, then the world's largest railcar manufacturer. Little did Pullman know that the plant in Longview would be used to build railcars to compete with Pullman, and that a few years later Trinity would wind up purchasing Pullman itself.

Trinity quickly built a 45,000-square-foot addition to the plant's 200,000-square-foot manufacturing space. The plant was located on a 54-acre site along a spur of the Missouri Pacific Railroad.[15]

A 4750 grain hopper car built by Trinity in 1981, shortly before the market collapsed. Richard Brown, who started the leasing business, is on the left.

Ray Wallace equated survival with growth, but he and the board of directors were nevertheless careful about acquisitions. At one point, the owners of a paint company offered to sell their concern to Trinity. Wallace brought the matter to the board's attention, and the company minutes noted "a major drawback." Buying a paint company would mean "entering a consumer-oriented market — an area in which the company has not previously been engaged," noted Wallace. "The board of directors was not particularly intrigued with the idea of entering into the paint manufacturing business, despite the fact that the company purchases approximately $1.5 million of paint each year."[16]

Besides both the Oklahoma City and Longview plants that were designated to build railcars, Trinity partly refitted four other plants to keep up with demand. A financial weekly reported in late 1979 that Trinity "on a capital investment of $35 to $40 million (more than $100 million, including inventories and receivables),... will be capable of turning out 8,000 cars a year."[17] Trinity's railcar sales for the fiscal year ended March 31, 1979, were $38.8 million.[18]

It was about this time that Trinity engineer Steve Smith saw the potential of a new design tool called computer-aided design, or CAD. When Smith was first hired, he followed simple instructions: Find a good design, copy it and then produce it more efficiently than the competition. Although Smith and Dick Martin had improved upon several car designs, notably the roofs of covered hopper cars, these were the exception.[19]

Smith knew that Trinity would eventually have to offer its own designs, and he saw the CAD system as the way to give the company's engineers an advantage. But in those days of hand-drafted designs, CAD systems were deemed expensive and were rare in the industry. Smith persisted. "My data was about a foot thick on this thing, and I still couldn't justify it," he said.

"At the time, I reported directly to Mr. [Ray] Wallace, and I was trying to work up the nerve to approach him about this. Four stations ran something like $250,000 to $300,000 in those days. But I knew there was a future in this. Well, he and I had a conversation, and he just said 'Keep looking at it.'"[20]

Then Wallace attended a board meeting in Redmond Plaza, where Trinity had rented some space. The owners of the plaza had bought a CAD system and were showing it off to Trinity's board. Wallace returned from the meeting and asked Smith, "Where's our CAD system? I feel like we're behind." A surprised Smith blurted, "You don't have to say another word."[21] Trinity was one of the first manufacturers in its industry to adopt such a system.

Cold-Starting the Leasing Business

With sales burgeoning in 1979, it was time for Trinity to develop a formal sales organization. Ray Wallace recruited a crack sales executive named Richard Brown to Trinity. Brown at the time was selling and leasing cars for Union Tank Car in Chicago, but he was interested in Trinity's flexibility in manufacturing. For about four months, he and Ray Wallace discussed his possible future with Trinity, and during the negotiations, Brown insisted that Trinity should lease both hopper and tank cars for the cash flow and tax advantage. Toward the end of their talks, Wallace asked him squarely: "Do you think you can sell the square ones as well as the round ones?" Brown replied he could and then asked if Wallace could build enough cars for him to sell. "I can build all the cars you can sell," asserted Wallace.[22]

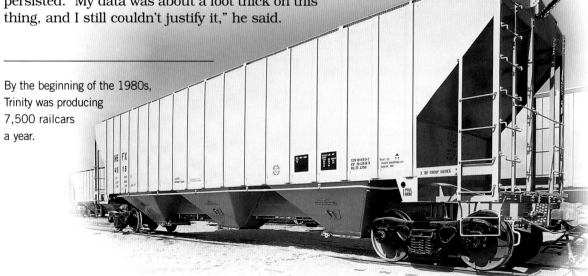

By the beginning of the 1980s, Trinity was producing 7,500 railcars a year.

Brown said he had another incentive to move from Chicago. After enduring years of the city's cold and snowy winters, his wife and children were ready to live in a more congenial climate.

When he started at Trinity that March, Brown had only his reputation to work with because Trinity possessed no formal sales organization and no direct marketing operation. But along with Brown came an order for 300 pressure cars. At this point, a debate erupted over whether to persuade the customer, Amoco, to lease these cars, a course Brown favored.

Amoco wanted to buy the cars outright. "So we negotiated and harangued and finally agreed to sell them 180 cars and lease the remaining order for 120 cars," recalled Brown. "That was the start of our lease fleet."[23]

By the end of his first year, the lease fleet grew to more than a thousand cars under the newly organized Trinity Industries Leasing Company and the Trinity Railcar Leasing Corporation. The leasing companies bought railroad cars, and later, river hopper barges manufactured by Trinity at market prices and then leased the equipment to third parties. Trinity initially owned 80 percent of Trinity Railcar Leasing as part of a joint venture — Trinity's first of that kind — with PLM, Inc., a West Coast equipment leasing firm. Trinity later purchased PLM's 20 percent interest.

The creation of the leasing subsidiaries was a good financial move. "Investment tax credits on railcars sold to the leasing subsidiaries were the primary reason for Trinity's lower corporate income tax rate of 21 percent — less than half the historical rate," reported Trinity's 1980 annual report. "Sales to the leasing subsidiaries also produced $13.8 million of deferred income, which the company will recognize over the life of the cars."[24]

In the meantime, the railcar business continued to flourish. By 1980, it was contributing more than 46 percent of Trinity's revenues. The company noted in its 1980 annual report that "thanks to Trinity's manufacturing flexibility, the company has become a substantial producer of finished railcars in less than two years.... We were able to enter the market in step with a surge in demand for railcars. By the end of the first full year of operations in March, we ranked among the top manufacturers of tank and hopper cars."[25]

By then, the company was making pressure and non-pressure tank cars, hopper cars and gondola cars at seven plants. The tank cars could carry such products as LPG, liquid fertilizer, sulfur, sulfuric acids and corn syrup. The covered hopper cars carried cargo such as grain, dry fertilizer and plastic pellets, while the open-top hoppers hauled coal. The gondolas carried heavy bulk items such as scrap metal, finished flat steel products and machinery.

Honored in Memory

C.J. Bender did not live to see Trinity succeed in yet another market. On May 10, 1977, the founder of Trinity Steel and longtime chairman of the board died at age 87. The company noted that "his wisdom and counsel will be missed. Our best memorial to his years of creative service will be the continued growth and vigor of Trinity Industries, Inc."[26] Bender was buried next to his wife Chummy in Hillcrest Memorial Park in Dallas. Even the funeral was classic Bender, recalled Trinity executive Lee McElroy, one of the pallbearers.

"I'll never forget this: We were carrying C.J. out of the church when a doggone squirrel jumped out of a tree right on top of the casket and sat there squealing at us. After it was all over with, I said, 'Well, C.J. had to do something for the boys.' Everybody roared laughing. We were all thinking the same thing."[27]

At the annual shareholders meeting, two months after Bender's death, stockholders honored him in resolutions. They also approved the placement of a memorial plaque at company offices.

At that same meeting, Ray Wallace outlined the company's accomplishments. He said that "out of all the top 1,000 industrial corporations in the United States, Trinity ranked 28th in total return to its investors for the 10-year period from 1966 to 1976.... Current assets are now 2.8 times greater than current liabilities."[28]

By the end of the decade, Trinity had achieved sales of $277 million, a 16 percent increase from the prior year. By March 1980, Trinity had increased its railcar production to an annual rate of more than 7,500 units.[29]

This 462-foot coal barge, built at Trinity's Ingalls shipyard in Alabama, has a niche fitted for a Halter Marine tugboat.

CHAPTER EIGHT
STEEL FORTITUDE

"Put me in the areas where the biggest challenges are so I can learn the most the fastest."

— Tim Wallace to his father, 1975[1]

TRINITY VICE PRESIDENT DON Graham remembered when he stood on the deck of the darkened *Andrew J. Barberi*, his heart pounding rapidly as the 310-foot Staten Island Ferry drifted slowly into the soft mud that extended several hundred feet from New York's Governors Island.

Nearby on the press boat, photographers and journalists crammed to one side snapping pictures as their craft scurried out of the way of the powerless *Barberi*. The journalists, he said, beseeched the captain of their vessel to keep as close as possible so they could capture the moment.[2]

The year was 1981, and the delivery of the ferry on that sundrenched August day was to be the successful culmination of more than four years of frustration for Trinity and the City of New York. The ferry was the first of two ordered by the city to replace the aging craft that plied passengers and cars regularly between Manhattan and Staten Island. Each of the new ferries, which together cost $31.5 million, could carry 6,000 people (sans their vehicles), double the number of the older vessels.[3]

In fact, the new design was meant to double as both a tourist attraction and a commuter service to and from Manhattan. The ferry sported a state-of-the-art German-made propulsion system designed to power the ferries sideways as well as forward and backward. Called cycloidal propulsion, the system replaced the obsolete steam-fired engines that,

besides their heavy maintenance requirements, performed poorly at low speeds. Rough currents shoved the ferries sideways into the interconnecting wooden pilings that bracket the ferry slips. The constant slamming and rubbing cost the city more than $1 million a year to replace damaged wood.[4]

This was the first debut of the propulsion system on a ferry in the United States and the first in so large a vessel. Equitable Shipyards engineers encountered basic design flaws that they had to work around. Delays ensued as the shipyard corrected the designs, and more delays ensued as Trinity tried to get the new designs approved by New York City officials. The first ferry was supposed to be delivered in 1979, but the decade ended with no end in sight to the engineering and contractual disputes. With the city verging on declaring Trinity in default of its contract, Ray Wallace put Graham and Tim Wallace in charge of the project. Graham handled the contractual problems, and Tim Wallace, who by then had become the acting president of Equitable, concentrated on getting the boats built without running too far in the red.[5]

The *Andrew Barberi* was the first of two Staten Island ferries built for New York City.

After a great deal of effort on both their parts, the first ferry was completed in the summer of 1981, and after several sea trials, the vessel began traveling under its own power from Louisiana to New York. On its trip, the *Andrew Barberi* had the occasion to render assistance to a boat in distress not far from Pensacola, Florida. While approaching, the *Barberi's* captain reported that two men began throwing bags — presumably filled with drugs — overboard. One can only imagine their reaction to being rescued by the clearly marked Staten Island Ferry.

The ferry's arrival in New York was cause for celebration. Fire boats sprayed streams of colored water, and Coast Guard helicopters and ships escorted the *Barberi* into the harbor with the press gathered to record the event. At the Staten Island dock, Mayor Edward Koch gave a speech to the crowd, which included local congressmen and members of the city council who were on hand to witness the fruit of their efforts and reap the credit — for 1982 was an election year.[6]

The captain delighted in showing off the craft. He demonstrated how the vessel could stop on a dime and crisply change directions, sideways as well as backwards and forwards. He neatly swung the boat into the dock, collected the passengers and began the short journey to Manhattan amid the parade of ships and helicopters. "All the dignitaries are on top of the four-story boat, and everyone's forgotten that it's two-and-a-half years late, and the rancorous process, with all the politicians who kept saying, 'This would never have happened on my beat,'" recalled Don Graham. "All is forgotten,

and everything is running perfectly with the World Trade Center in the background and two press boats running alongside. Loaded with cameras."[7]

They were just passing Governors Island when Graham noticed that the captain, inside the wheelhouse, was alternately shaking his head, shrugging his shoulders and gesticulating with his hands. Graham looked aft and realized that the boat's wake was no longer straight.

In the wheelhouse, the captain flatly told him, "We've lost all power."[8]

For three minutes the boat drifted into the mud off the island. A member of the crew grabbed an ax and was preparing to cut the anchor loose when one of the representatives from the German company had an idea. He went to the circuit box and reset one of the breakers. As power came back on, the captain righted the boat's path, Graham's heart returned to something resembling normal rhythm, and they made it to Manhattan without further incident.

Graham rushed off the boat to let Ray Wallace know the outcome. Up to that point, Wallace had heard nothing but good news since the ferry made its way to New York, a welcome change from the financial, legal and technical headaches that the project had caused. His first words to Graham were, "Congratulations!"

Graham had to tell him what had actually transpired, but Wallace didn't get upset; he just said to get this latest problem fixed. The second ferry, the *Samuel I. Newhouse*, was delivered in June 1982 without incident.

Barging Forward

As unpleasant as it was, the ferryboat experience was the exception that year at Trinity because the barge business was reaping handsome profits. Trinity, one of about 12 barge manufacturers in the United States, was on its way to becoming North America's leading producer of the craft. In 1980, for instance, Equitable's shipyard at Madisonville was turning out about six barges a week, and the New Orleans yard was gearing up to produce an additional three barges a week.

For fiscal 1981, the results of Trinity's marine products business were nothing short of spectacular. From an operating loss of $2.4 million on sales of $52.3 million in fiscal 1980, the shipyard brought in an operating profit of $11 million on sales of $134.7 million in fiscal 1981.[9] The nation's shipyards were benefiting from a strong demand for barges since inland waterways were the least expensive way to move bulk cargo like grain, fertilizer and coal. Trinity, during that year, had further penetrated the barge market with its line of river hopper barges, a product line Tim Wallace had been setting up before he was directed to concentrate on the Staten Island Ferry project.

Opposite: Unlike the *Barberi*, the delivery of the *Samuel I. Newhouse* to New York City went relatively smoothly.

Below: Halter Marine built the 1,000-passenger *Creole Queen* at its Moss Point shipyard in Mississippi. A New Orleans tourist attraction, the ship specialized in three-hour river cruises.

The barge market had many similarities to the railcar market. Both areas had been neglected for some years, so replacements were sorely needed; both were affected by the same trends (foreign grain deals and a rapidly growing chemical industry prodded the need for hopper and tank barges, respectively); and both were eligible to be used as a tax shelter. Trinity first built hopper barges and later moved into tank barge construction following the acquisitions of Ingalls Iron Works of Decatur, Alabama, and Gretna Machine and Iron Works, located in Harvey, Louisiana. Both the Ingalls and Gretna acquisitions permitted Trinity to supply ocean barges that were designed to match the tugboats built by Halter Marine, which would soon become another Trinity acquisition.[10]

The purchase of these two companies expanded existing markets and launched Trinity into new businesses. Ingalls, for instance, produced plate and structural steel, did structural steel erection and built tank barges for the petrochemical and petroleum industries. Ingalls had shipyards in Alabama and Georgia, plus 24 plants in nine states, with sales of nearly $145 million in 1979.[11]

Until it purchased Ingalls Iron Works, Trinity did not erect steel or build tank barges. Ingalls' location opened up wider geographical areas, namely the Eastern and Southeastern United States. Its management and marketing functions for structural products and metal components were combined with those of Mosher Steel, while Ingalls' marine operations were reorganized into a new company called Ingalls Marine, Inc. Trinity sold off Ingalls' steel service centers because they did not complement Trinity's mission.

A 162,000-barrel-capacity oil transport barge built at Gretna. Gretna was a pioneer in the development of oceangoing barges.

The purchase of Gretna, meanwhile, gave Trinity a fifth shipyard. Wallace told board members that "its potential to the company is the cleaning of railcars and barges in which it is one of the pioneer companies."[12] The facility, in addition to manufacturing oceangoing tank barges at a 47-acre leased yard on the Harvey Canal, boasted one of the most modern tank-barge repair and cleaning operations in existence, with equipment to remove all residue from a tank barge and on-site storage facilities for waste chemicals. The waste was sold to a refinery for reprocessing.[13] Ray Wallace had another reason behind Gretna's purchase. He wanted to acquire its vice president and general manager, George J. Fegert.[14] Fegert continued to be in charge of the plant and became its president.

The acquisitions catapulted Trinity to *Fortune* 500 status in 1981. With revenues of $515 million, the company rose from number 632 to number 467 on the list and ranked third in total return to investors between 1970 and 1980. Trinity also ranked 24th in return on shareholders' equity for the 1980 fiscal year and 37th in earnings-per-share growth for the last 10 years.[15]

Trinity's marine products segment had another great year in 1982. Its operating profit contributed $29.3 million on sales of $202 million, and the company was supplying more than 12 percent of the 2,600 barges built nationwide.[16]

Railcars, the biggest single source of revenue, had gone on a steep decline, but barge sales more than made up for the downturn. At its peak, the company was turning out 15 to 17 barges a week, each with a price tag of around $300,000.[17]

Like railcars, barges were an ideal addition to the lease fleet. By 1981, the leasing company had 41 barges under contract, and the numbers continued to grow apace with railcars.[18] That number was destined to soar quickly into the hundreds. In April of that year, A.W. Kersteter became president of Ingalls Marine, Inc. In December, Tim Wallace recommended that Archibald Dunn, formerly vice president of Litton Industries' Ingalls Shipbuilding, take over Equitable. Wallace was already looking ahead to his next challenge.

Collapse of the Railcar Market

When Tim Wallace entered the company as a full-time employee, he and his father made the same pact that Ray had made with his uncle: "You know I'm not going to fire you, and I know you're not going to quit." Tim had a second agreement with his father: "Put me in the areas where the biggest challenges are so I can learn the most the fastest," which amounted to the jobs that no one else wanted to do or that presented the most problems.[19] After his tenure at Equitable, which was the younger Wallace's first experience at running a business, he moved on to handle cost control for the company in 1982.

Ray Wallace kept his word to his son because it was at this time that the railcar business crashed with the screeching suddenness and metal-wrenching cataclysm associated with a train wreck. After absorbing an astounding 96,000 railcars in 1980 (a feat never accomplished before or since), the market was saturated. In 1983, just 5,800 railcars were delivered to customers.[20] By comparison, an average "up" year for man-ufacturers throughout the 1970s was somewhere around 65,000 new cars built, and a "down" year meant about 35,000 units.[21] The binge was over; now was the time for the hangover.

Compounding the misery was President Carter's suspension of grain sales to the Soviet Union in retaliation for its invasion of Afghanistan in 1980. The embargo and the recession — with inflation scraping the sky at 17 percent — idled more than 20 percent of covered hopper cars.[22] The last nail was the elimination of the 10 percent tax credit that had made railcars so attractive in the first place.

When the market cratered, there were about 28 freight car builders vying for a piece of a pie that no longer existed. Companies without a significant lease fleet were the hardest hit; Pullman Standard, which had been the biggest freight car builder in the nation, shut down entirely. Others stayed half-alive by subsisting on repair work.

Trinity's top revenue producer had been its railcar segment. In 1981, just prior to the collapse, the railcar segment brought in almost $345 million, which made up close to half of that year's total revenue of $736 million. The earnings were even more sweet; in one year, from 1980 to 1981, income had doubled to $62.4 million.[23] That streak ended in fiscal 1983. Its railcar segment plummeted

THE INGALLS LEGACY

T HE INGALLS STEEL AND SHIPBUILD-
ing empire began in 1911 when Robert
Ingalls bought his partners out for
$5,000 and became sole proprietor of a small
machine shop in Birmingham, Alabama. He
was soon producing a variety of high-quality
products such as ornamental iron and steel
grating, fire escapes and stairways.[1]

The company's rise was rapid. During World
War I, Ingalls created the Steel Construction
Company to erect its steel, and after the war, it
created a tank and plate fabricating facility
called The Birmingham Tank Company. The
tank company, according to an Ingalls magazine, "was one of the first companies to use the
all-welded process of tank construction."[2]

Ingalls Iron Works grew even during
the Great Depression, when its Verona,
Pennsylvania, plant became a major structural
steel supplier. In 1936, Ingalls founded the
Ingalls Marine Division on the Tennessee
River at Decatur, where he pioneered the construction of all-welded vessels. World War II
accelerated these efforts, and the division continued to innovate in the design and construction of large inland and oceangoing barges of
all types.[3] Ingalls also had a small yard at
Chickasaw, Alabama, where the company
built America's first all-welded tanker in 1936.[4]

The shipbuilding portion of this empire
came from the interests of Ingalls' son, Robert,
Jr. "Young Bob, a shipbuilding buff since his
early teens, had persuaded his father to take a
flyer in barge construction some years before,"
reported *Fortune* magazine.

*"The [marine division] and the small yard at
Chickasaw, Alabama,... had turned out more
profitably than the ironworks itself. Thus the
old man's eyes were opened wide enough so
that by 1938, after the government had
announced its bold new program of building*

*50 ships a year for 10 years, he was ready to
bid — provided, of course, it wouldn't cost him
anything much."[5]*

The shipyard won contracts to build four
C3 cargo ships and built a shipyard large
enough to handle the 12,500-ton vessels.
Ingalls built the ships and the shipyard virtually
at the same time.[6]

The shipyard and iron works that supplied
its steel prospered during World War II and in
the Cold War aftermath, but the family in
charge of the sprawling million-dollar empire

Robert I. Ingalls, founder of Ingalls Iron Works, went into
shipbuilding at the insistence of his son. *(Photo courtesy
of the Birmingham Public Library.)*

had been torn asunder. In a 1952 article, *Time* magazine reported that "when ruggedly individualistic Robert Ingersoll Ingalls, Sr. died last year at 68, he left behind a double legacy: a $40 million, family-controlled iron and shipbuilding empire, and a bitter legal wrangle over who should run it."[7]

Ingalls' only son, Robert, Jr., had become president of the Iron Works in 1941. According to *Time* magazine, the elder Ingalls, a "stern Presbyterian," became angry over his son's divorce and remarriage and fired Robert, Jr. seven years later from his $45,000-a-year job, setting off legal actions and bitter recriminations.[8] The family dispute continued after the death of the elder Ingalls.

In 1961, Robert, Jr., sold his interest in Ingalls to a group headed by William H. Hulsey, president of a mortgage and insurance agency, who then sold the shipyard to California-based Litton Industries Inc.

Meanwhile, Ingalls Iron Works had grown from four steel fabricating companies in 1965 to more than 25 operating companies nearly a decade later.

A company pamphlet from the late 1970s sketched out some of the company's accomplishments and expertise. At that time, 50 per-cent of Ingalls' capacity was devoted to serving the energy industry. It constructed both nuclear and fossil fuel power plants. The company also contributed to the construction of many bridges, office buildings, sports arenas and stadiums, including Shea Stadium in New York, Riverfront Stadium in Cincinnati and Atlanta Stadium in Atlanta. Ingalls even supplied and erected the steel for the three Apollo Launch Umbilical Towers, used throughout the moon program and later in the space shuttle program. It was one of the few companies that could construct and transport girders weighing more than 300 tons.

Ingalls' tank and plate products included pressure vessels, storage tanks, stoves, blast furnaces and tank heads for LP gas barges. The company custom-built cargo vessels to carry petroleum products and chemicals as well as dry commodities such as grain and coal. And it could build oceangoing barges up to 600 feet long and 105 feet wide.

More than 4,000 tons of steel fabricated at Ingalls' Birmingham and Verona plants went into this all-welded aircraft carrier, shown in 1943.

through the floor and into the basement, bottoming out that year at $34 million in sales.

Streamlining

Unlike the rest of the industry, however, Trinity continued to produce railcars, demonstrating that the company was outperforming its competitors.[24] In charge of keeping Trinity's Railcar Division viable, Tim Wallace helped to centralize purchasing, cut down on waste and duplication, and do more with less.

"I wrote a whole series of cost-control bulletins on the best way of buying welding wire, the best way of buying janitorial supplies, the best way of buying paint, whatever it was. Anything we bought in bulk, we researched and tried to find ways of cutting our cost."[25]

As part of its cost cutting, Trinity discontinued operations at some plants, selling or leasing the real estate and equipment. Accounting work was consolidated in Dallas, and employees who had been in leased space elsewhere in Dallas were moved to the main offices at Irving Boulevard or to the Mosher plant on Maple Avenue in Dallas. Some people were laid off. The company also simplified its corporate structure by merging all of its subsidiaries, except the leasing and transportation operations, into the parent. Trinity continued to use the well-known names of Mosher, Gambles, Ingalls, Hackney,

A tank car approaches final assembly in Longview, Texas. The market was almost at a standstill and orders were few and far between, but Trinity continued to build railcars.

Equitable and Gretna, but as operating divisions, not subsidiaries.

New federal regulations had been enacted to boost the railroad economy. Railroads were given more pricing flexibility and the authority to negotiate contract rates. Regulations were loosened with the passage of the Staggers Rail Act of 1980, which removed significant amounts of governmental regulations on pricing and railroad mergers. The law helped spark competition and restructure the industry by abetting the startup of hundreds of new short-line and regional railroads. Deregulation was a break that would benefit the railroads and, ultimately, manufacturers like Trinity.

Halter Marine

Trinity had taken a two-year hiatus from its acquisitions strategy. In 1983, it returned with a vengeance, wrapping up the major acquisitions of Halter Marine and the virtually defunct Pullman Standard within nine days of each other. With these acquisitions Trinity obtained designs and markets it previously did not have access to. Of the two, Halter Marine was the larger. In fact, Halter was the largest acquisition Trinity made that year. It was also the more risky, for Trinity was diverging from its traditional manufacturing expertise. With the possible exception of structural products, Trinity had, for the most part, staked its success on the ability to build repetitive products — barges, railcars and guardrails, for instance — more efficiently than its competitors. Many of Halter's products, however, were special-order items, designs that changed from customer to customer.

Halter Marine was the nation's largest builder of support vessels for the offshore oil and gas industry, a business segment already served by Trinity's shipyards. Trinity principally built barges that were often fitted to boats built by Halter Marine.

Trinity bought Halter Marine toward the tail end of the barge boom. The privately owned ship-

yard had recorded annual revenues of about $190 million when it was purchased, and Ed Breeding, a Trinity senior vice president, noted in an interview that the shipyard was "like everyone else right now, hunting for business. That's part of the reason we were able to buy them."[26]

Halter Marine owned six shipyards, three of which were in the New Orleans area. The supplier of almost half of the world's offshore service and exploration vessels, Halter was the nation's leader in diesel-electric propulsion based on silicon-controlled rectifiers, the most efficient technology with which to search for oil and gas in deep waters and harsh climates like the biting cold and rolling waves of the North Sea. The diesel-electric propulsion system gave operators absolute control over the vessels' engines from zero RPM to maximum RPM, which was not possible in conventional systems.[27]

Along with the acquisition came Halter Marine's minority interest in Bell Halter, Inc., a New Orleans joint venture between Halter Marine and

The *Point Bravo*, a 192-foot tug and supply boat that served offshore drilling platforms in the Gulf of Mexico, was built by Halter Marine.

HALTER MARINE: RIDING THE WAVES

THE IDEA BEHIND HALTER MARINE began in Korea, where Harold P. Halter served in the army during the Korean War. Afterward, Halter launched his idea in his backyard, working in the evenings and on weekends, when not at his job in a maintenance department at a machine shop.

Halter had the idea to build a steel-hulled pleasure boat, which he called the Sea Cat model. His goal was modest, calling for a workforce of only about 25 employees to build the yachts. Enlisting the help of a friend, he built the first boat only to discover that the market wasn't ready for steel-hulled yachts. The offshore oil industry, however, was a different matter, as Halter told the *Times-Picayune*:

> *"I was looking at the offshore industry developing and trying to get a feel for it, so I decided to switch from the pleasure boats to the steel crew boats. At that time, there was a big market for 31- and 36-footers, and I got a contract for a $14,000 boat. I quit my job at the machine shop and bought two lots.... I put up a little building out there and decided to get with it."[1]*

The company first produced all-steel crew boats. Then, sometime in 1960, Halter Marine began building steel-hulled, aluminum-cabined craft. Within several years, Halter was making all-aluminum boats and then expanded into such vessels as offshore work boats and river pushboats.[2] By 1976, Halter Marine employed 1,500 workers in six yards and was delivering 49 percent of the world's supply boats, ranging between 100 feet and 217 feet. In 1980, the company delivered its 1,000th vessel in less than 25 years of boatbuilding and was the world's largest builder of support vessels for the offshore oil and gas industry.[3]

By this time, Harold Halter felt nothing but optimism, and he had the figures to back it up. Oil exploration continued to drive his revenues upwards, jumping 54 percent from the previous year to $200 million, and the company had taken its first steps into vessels for transocean shipping by building seven catamaran tugboats. The 18,000-horsepower tugboats, which were large vessels with twin or catamaran hulls, could be linked with huge barges to form integrated tug-barges. The result: an ocean tanker 688 feet long, in two pieces. The barges were being built by Bethlehem Steel and other companies. Halter Marine was building the catamaran tugboats, or Catugs, at its Chickasaw, Alabama, yard.

But the world oil market had begun an uncomfortable rumbling. OPEC (the Organization of Petroleum Exporting Countries) had lost control of production, two of the oil cartel's members were at war and a lingering recession slackened worldwide demand. The conditions spelled doom for many of the drilling operations that were Halter's best customers.

To make matters worse, the federal government reduced subsidies and ended the loan-guarantee program that had spurred the building of these craft, no longer allowing barges to be used as tax shelters. The lingering recession and the slack demand for barges and other craft had a devastating effect on the marine industry. Halter's employment at the end of 1981 had peaked at 3,000. By the time Trinity bought Halter Marine in late 1983, an industry observer estimated that employment at the New Orleans company had shrunk to 700, and the company had withdrawn entirely from the pleasure boat market.[4]

the Bell Aerospace Division of Textron, Inc. The joint venture built a variety of hovercraft, including air cushion vessels and surface-effect ships, under commercial and military contracts. The surface-effect ships were similar in nature to catamarans and were built for the U.S. Coast Guard and the U.S. Navy, as well as for commercial interests in the Gulf of Mexico. Such vessels significantly reduced operating costs because of their lower fuel consumption. Capable of speeds up to 70 knots, they were used for urban and inter-island passenger ferries and offshore support vessels — such as crew boats, fireboats, hydrographic survey boats and high-speed military patrol boats.[28]

Halter Marine also had experience in building boats for foreign nations. Saudi Arabia in 1976 awarded Halter Marine a contract worth an estimated $6 million to build a dozen 50-foot patrol boats. The boats were used for customs, police and coastal patrol. The contract was the first such commercial pact between Saudi Arabia and a United States shipyard. Later contracts for similar patrol boats were signed with governments that included Taiwan and Guatemala.

Structural Products

The need to reduce costs was amplified by Trinity's sales and income, both of which were down in fiscal 1983. Once again, income had fallen by more than half from the previous fiscal year (from $39 million in fiscal 1982 to $16.5 million in fiscal 1983). Total revenue had likewise fallen to $477 million. In addition to a saturated railcar market, the marine business had fallen off because of high interest rates, the change in tax laws, a depressed agricultural industry and fewer housing starts.

The structural products segment shined brightly, however, especially with down cycles slamming the other business segments. Sales for structural products had risen a gratifying 42 percent in 1983 from the previous year. The Sunbelt was enjoying a population boost from people seeking to thaw out from several bitter winters. The South was also in the midst of a boom in high-rise commercial construction, and there was a strong demand for power-generating plants. Trinity also undertook

providing the supply of steel for a full-scale coal gasification plant, as well as for a number of electric power and industrial plants.

Trinity — through its divisions of Mosher, Gambles and Ingalls — had become the largest supplier of structural products in the United States. A recent increase in the federal gasoline tax, earmarked to pay for refurbishing the nation's aging highways, was expected to fuel more sales of steel for bridges and highway guardrails.

With railcar and barge production in decline, structural products became Trinity's largest business segment in 1982 and 1983. The company shipped some 20,000 tons of steel to build a new General Motors plant in Detroit and 16,000 tons for an office building in Mexico for Petroleos Mexicanos, or PEMEX. In Houston, it provided 29,000 tons of steel for the Allied Bank Plaza building.[29] The company had strengthened its metal components portfolio by purchasing the fittings and forging division of Babcock & Wilcox Company, a move that expanded Trinity's capacity and product mix.[30]

A highly automated plate roll machine in a Fort Worth plant forms a shell section for a large container.

The company also purchased a rare hot-forming head machine, one of only two in the United States, from Bethlehem Steel. The equipment could form steel heads up to 20 feet in diameter. The steel heads were used on processing vessels for chemical and petrochemical companies. In the coming years, these mighty machines would handle loads of up to 54,000 pounds.

In 1983, Trinity purchased three structural products fabricators: AESCO Steel, Inc., of Montgomery, Alabama; General Steel; and Industrial Steel Products, Inc.[31] AESCO, an acronym formed from its original name, Alabama Engineering and Supply Company, made plate and structural steel. Fort Worth–based General Steel provided steel for buildings and power plants, and Industrial Steel Products was located in Shreveport, Louisiana. This Gulf Coast facility supplied Trinity with plate steel in coiled form, which is less expensive on a tonnage basis.

AESCO had grown to rival Gambles, and in fact one of its founders, Cecil Spear, had worked for Alf Gamble years before Gamble sold his business to Trinity and became one of its directors. "I'd say if you came to Alabama, that probably 95 percent of the steel structures that you'd ride on were either furnished by Gambles or AESCO, and Gambles did the most of them," Spear said.[32]

AESCO supplied steel for bridges along the interstate highway system in Alabama and for the headquarters of the publishers of *Southern Living* magazine in Birmingham. The latter project was constructed out of a weathering steel developed by the industry called Cor-Ten. AESCO also fabricated the steel used in the test towers for the Saturn V rocket project at the Redstone Arsenal in Huntsville, Alabama, as well as for the Orange County Civic Center in Orlando, Florida.

By the end of the year, Trinity's newest acquisitions had sent the Structural Products Division's net income spiraling upward, from $8 million the prior year to $22 million. Revenue had risen over the same period from $238 million to almost $338 million.

Romance and Railroads

Just nine days after the purchase of Halter Marine, Ray Wallace announced the acquisition of a legacy. With the purchase of the assets and designs of Pullman Standard (for all practical purposes a defunct subsidiary of Pullman Transportation), Trinity was on its way to becoming the nation's largest railcar builder just five short years after the company entered the fray. It was buying a company that had once been the largest, and was certainly the oldest, maker of sleeper and freight cars.

Trinity purchased Pullman Standard for $25 million in cash and notes. Pullman's plants in Butler, Pennsylvania, and Bessemer, Alabama, fell under Trinity's control, as did a freight car parts plant located in Asheville, North Carolina, and a test center in Hammond, Indiana. Unlike the facilities

A Trinity worker installs tubes in a heat exchanger tube bundle.

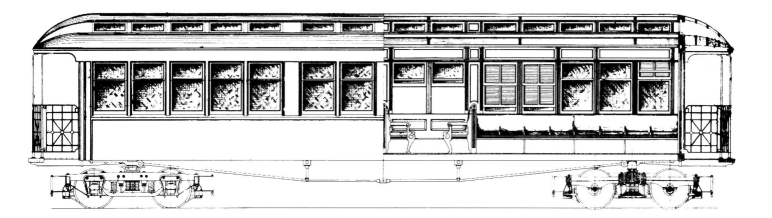

in Butler and Bessemer, the Asheville plant was still viable; it continued to produce trailer hitches for intermodal flat cars and other railcar parts.

Pullman Standard had shut down the Butler and Bessemer plants in 1981, even before the railcar crisis hit in full force. The biggest victim of the recession, Pullman Standard, had already been sliced up. "There were a lot of folks that were taking advantage of the heartaches, and they would buy a company and then sell it off," Ray Wallace explained. "They could buy it on the market for almost nothing and sell the pieces off and make a fortune. That happened across the board in the railcar industry."[33] There was more left at Pullman Standard, however, than empty machine shops and a few leftover people in the engineering department. Prior to its closing as a commercial venture, Pullman Standard had built a few prototype intermodal cars and one all-aluminum coal car, noted the magazine *Railway Age*.

"The real assets for Trinity appeared to be the designs, and the rights to manufacture and market them in North and South America. Pullman's intermodal prototypes have proved out well; its aluminum high-side gondola for coal (developed in cooperation with Alcoa) is looking good even though tests will not be completed until next month — and the rest of the Pullman portfolio used to be a standard in the industry. In addition, the Asheville component plant has been a profit-maker."[34]

"This was a once-in-a-lifetime opportunity," noted Ken Lewis, who would succeed Ed Breeding

A Pullman Standard car from 1886. Once king of the tracks, the company fell on hard times and was gradually broken up and sold off.

as CFO in 1986. "To buy all the assets for what we did was remarkable." As the article noted, the Pullman acquisition gave Trinity exclusive licensing to manufacture and market in the Western Hemisphere all Pullman-designed freight cars, including new designs for intermodal cars and aluminum coal cars.[36]

Trinity still had to weather the worst conditions for the market since the Great Depression.[35] Indeed, railway equipment suppliers, noting their interdependence with the railroads, testified before Congress in the fall of 1983 that they had been in "increasingly serious trouble for the past two years." Unemployment in the railway supply industry ran close to 62 percent.[37] Railcar production had plunged to 150 cars a month in June 1983 from a 1981 monthly high of about 2,000.[38]

Expectations were that the railcar fleet would require replacements and new designs sometime in the late 1980s. The recovery took longer than the industry anticipated, but Ray Wallace was confident that "the combination of Pullman's designs with our manufacturing expertise opens up tremendous future potential for Trinity."[39] With Pullman Standard, Trinity, the young upstart in railcars, had acquired more than 130 years of experience and one of the most romantic names in the history of railroading.

Passenger cars await completion at an unidentified Pullman Standard yard. Pullman Standard dominated both passenger and freight car production throughout the golden age of railroads. (*Photo courtesy of the California State Railroad Museum Library.*)

CHAPTER NINE

THE PULLMAN STANDARD STORY

"George Pullman came to be remembered as an inventor, which he was not; rather, he was an astute businessman who sold his generation sumptuous and comfortable railroad accommodations."

— from *A Biography of George Mortimer Pullman*[1]

TRINITY'S PURCHASE OF Pullman Standard in 1983 was the latest in a series of upheavals for Pullman Standard. Since 1979, when Pullman halted production of its famed passenger cars, it had been bought, sold and bought again. It was a dizzying spiral of changes for a company that was rooted in American railroad lore.

The seeds for the company were planted in Illinois in 1867, two years after the Civil War, when George Mortimer Pullman organized Pullman Palace Car Company to build and operate his famous sleeping cars and other types of railway cars. Contrary to legend, Pullman did not invent the sleeper car. According to Peter T. Maiken, author of *Night Trains: The Pullman System in the Golden Years of American Travel*, Pullman "simply took a good idea, built upon it, and shrewdly turned it into the most remarkable transportation system in the world. Simple testimony, it would seem, to the notion that if you can't be the first, be the best."[2]

A Comfortable Train of Thought

Pullman was born March 3, 1831, in New York state. He left school at 14, clerked in a general store and later worked in a cabinet-making shop. His father, Lewis, a carpenter, had acquired a patent in 1841 for inventing a machine for transporting buildings upon wheels. With his

father's illness and then death in 1853, Pullman took over his father's house-moving firm and the support of his mother and younger siblings.[3]

It was Pullman's frequent train rides that led him to realize the importance of comfortable travel. Pullman rode the night train between Westfield and Buffalo, New York, a distance of about 60 miles. He endured the discomforts, fatigue and indignities that were the standard fare of modern train travel. "He tossed and turned on the narrow wooden bunk, fully dressed even to boots and topcoat as was the custom of that day," noted a 1955 Pullman magazine. "As he did so, he thought longingly of sheets and pillow, and of the comforts of a mattress. Out of this nightmare trip came the germ of an idea which took root several years later. And once he started to work on his idea it grew by leaps and bounds. The idea began a train of thought which reached around the globe."[4]

In 1858, Pullman hired Leonard Seibert, an employee on the Chicago & Alton Railroad, to remodel two of that railroad's passenger coaches

---

Cleveland's 70-foot air-conditioned airport car with special luggage racks and wide double doors. In later years, the passenger car market became a financial drain on the company.

into the first Pullman sleeping cars. Seibert, in *The Story of the Pullman Car*, recalled the specifics of the remodeling.

> "We selected Coaches Nos. 9 and 19. They were 44 feet long, had flat roofs like box cars, single sash windows, of which there were 14 on a side, the glass in each sash being only a little over one foot square. The roof was only a trifle over six feet from the floor of the car. Into this car we got 10 sleeping-car sections, besides a linen locker and two washrooms.... There were no blue-prints or plans made for the remodeling of these first two sleeping-cars, and Mr. Pullman and I worked out the details and measurements as we came to them. The two cars cost Mr. Pullman ... $1,000 each. They were upholstered in plush, lighted by oil lamps, heated with box stoves and mounted on four-wheel trucks with iron wheels."[5]

In 1865, Pullman used his savings to build a sleeping car from scratch in a shed belonging to the Chicago & Alton Railroad in Chicago. The *Pioneer* became the stuff of legends. Traditional accounts say its total cost of $20,000 to build and outfit was four times that of an ordinary coach and that it was used in President Lincoln's funeral train in 1865. No photographs of the original *Pioneer* are known to exist. The car was remodeled several times before its demolition in 1903. One writer described its interior as ornate:

> "Costly brocaded fabrics covered the seats and seat backs; beautifully matched woods of exotic grain were worked into door frames, windows and panels at the ends of the car itself. Coal-oil lamps were trimmed in silver and there was a profusion of mirrors which reflected their light in dimensions that seemed actually palatial. On the floor the red Turkey carpet discouraged spitting and the bed linen was the finest that Pullman could buy."[6]

In 1866, five Pullman sleeping cars were rolling on the Chicago, Burlington & Quincy Railroad. By

the next year, Pullman owned all the sleeping cars on the Michigan Central Railroad, Great Western (Canada) Railroad and New York Central Railroad lines, a total of 48 cars.[7] The year 1867 was also when he incorporated the company as Pullman Palace Car Company and when Pullman's first "hotel car" began service on the Great Western Railroad of Canada. The hotel car was a sleeping car with a built-in kitchen at one end and tables for the meals placed in the car's sections, making Pullman the first to supply the public with meals aboard trains.[8]

In 1880, George Pullman created an industrial center and namesake community 15 miles south of Chicago near Lake Calumet. The town of Pullman was America's first planned industrial community and in it lived the workers of the red-brick Pullman Car Works. The factory buildings were located in the center of the town, while the industrial center was dominated by the Administration and Clock Tower building. Most of the homes were row houses, fashioned from brick produced from the blue clay of the lake, and the town included schools, stores, churches, a theater and a hotel. Power for the town came from the 700-ton Corliss engine, which had run the 1876 Philadelphia Centennial Exposition. By the early 1890s, the town's population reached 11,800.[9]

George Pullman remained president of Pullman Palace Car Company for 30 years, until his death in 1897.[10] Robert Todd Lincoln, son of President Lincoln, succeeded Pullman as president, serving in that role for a dozen years and then taking over as chairman of the board. In 1899, the company's name was simplified to The Pullman Company, and it bought the Wagner Palace Car Company, which had been providing sleeping cars to the New York Central and other railroads.[11]

Opposite page, above: The Pullman *Pioneer* sleeping car after several remodelings. Photos of the original car are said not to exist.

Opposite page, below: George Pullman's sleeping cars achieved the height of luxury for the well-heeled traveler. (*Photos courtesy of the California State Railroad Museum Library.*)

Moving Freight

In the shadow of the luxurious passenger cars, Pullman also built freight cars. By 1892, production had reached 40 cars a day, with 21,134 of its freight cars on the tracks. The types of cars ranged from boxcars to cabooses to coal and poultry cars.[12]

Pullman had switched from wood to metal cars during this period, an innovation that was hastened by the opening of the Pennsylvania Railroad tunnel under the Hudson River. The railroad banned wood cars because they were a fire hazard, so Pullman relied on metal for both freight and passenger cars.[13]

In 1921, Pullman bought Haskell & Barker Car Company, based in Michigan City, Indiana, and became the largest manufacturer of passenger and freight cars in the world. Haskell & Barker had been formed in 1852 to build wagons and railway cars and had the capacity to build more than 20,000 wood and steel railway cars a year.[14] With the merger, Edward Carry, president of Haskell & Barker, was named president of the combined firm, replacing the retiring Pullman president, J.S. Runnels, who became chairman of the board.[15]

Haskell & Barker was one of the first railcar builders to use a straight-line production track. Previously, cars were assembled in one place in what was called the "stall method." However, a fire that destroyed the company's main shops inadvertently "caused the birth of mass production methods in carbuilding which were copied by automobile factories 10 or more years later," according to an industry publication.[16] Before construction began on a replacement shop, the workers themselves asked the company why it was clinging to old methods.

"'Why can't we eliminate the crowding of men and materials around the stalls? Why not start with the trucks at one end of a railroad track inside the building, and pull those wheels a car length at a time? At each stop we can add the next component. By the time we bolt on the roof, the car will be ready to go to the paint building. With cars hitched to one another we will be producing more than ever before.' And so it was that the new building was fitted for America's first straight-line production track."[17]

In 1929, Pullman built a plant in Bessemer, Alabama, about 12 miles west of Birmingham. The 16-building plant used some equipment and buildings that Pullman bought from the Chickasaw Shipbuilding and Car Company near Fairfield. By January 1930, three months after the grand opening, workers built and delivered 600 box cars to the National Railways of Mexico. "This was the beginning of a period in time in which the Bessemer plant was one of the most efficient and largest producers of freight cars and parts in the country. There was constant production of freight cars of all types — box, automobile, hopper, gondola, cement, phosphate and flat cars."[18]

Later that year Pullman purchased the Standard Steel Company and the Osgood Bradley Car Company, giving it car facilities in Hammond, Indiana, and Butler, Pennsylvania; wheel foundries at Michigan City, Houston and New Orleans; a passenger-car plant at Worcester, Massachusetts; and two overseas possessions that Standard had controlled — a freight works in Rio de Janeiro and a passenger-car works in France.[19]

Pullman dominated the freight car business as thoroughly as it did the passenger car business.

Out of the total 65,349 freight cars built in 1930, 21,715 were Pullman. The Great Depression quickly stopped production almost entirely, however. In 1932, the Depression's worst year, Pullman built just 252 freight cars, and that number was more than half of what was built nationwide.[20]

In 1934, Pullman Standard Car Manufacturing Company was formed to consolidate the railroad interests of what in 1927 had been organized as Pullman, Inc., a holding company. As economic conditions improved, the federal government took an active interest in the company. In 1940, the Justice Department slapped Pullman Standard with an antitrust suit, accusing the company of creating a monopoly because it built and operated sleeper cars. The suit was put on hold for World War II, but seven years later the company was forced to sell The Pullman Company, which operated the sleeper service.[21]

The plant in Bessemer, Alabama, achieved distinction as one of the largest and most efficient railcar facilities in the nation. *(Photo courtesy of the Birmingham Public Library.)*

Serving Its Country

During the war, railroads became the lifeline of transportation. Gas rationing had reduced automobile travel, and air traffic had been cut, so it was up to the railroads to transport troops, equipment, raw materials and civilian war workers. This was a prosperous time for Pullman, which also converted some of its plants to building sections of warships because shipbuilding called for essentially the same welding process.[22]

At the Butler plant, workers forged 7 million artillery shells, along with thousands of rockets and bombs, and turned out freight cars for both military and domestic use.[23] At the Bessemer plant, workers built bomb casings as well as boxcars and cabooses for the Army's use overseas. During a frenzy of manufacturing, on July 13, 1943, the Bessemer plant reached an all-time high per day of 50 boxcars for military use and 18 domestic hopper cars. Even after the war, the plant continued its fast pace, turning out a record 1,208 domestic freight cars in December 1948.[24]

But with the end of the war came a decline in railroad passenger and freight traffic. Despite increased efficiency, streamlining and piggyback service, railroads were fighting what seemed like a losing battle with the "convenience of the truck, the speed of the airline, the economy of the bus, and the cheap reliability of the pipeline," wrote railroad historian John Stover.[25]

Evolving with the Times

Thus, Pullman began to move to standardized cars to cut the costs of railcars. After the war, it developed the PS-1 boxcar, which made its debut in 1947. During 1954, the PS-1 design accounted for 85 percent of all boxcars shipped.[26] Other standardized hopper and passenger cars followed.

Pullman also had adopted new business practices. In 1961, in its freight car-building division, "it created a department of industrial marketing staffed largely with young men who were to work with shippers to determine their needs for specialized cars," noted *Forbes* magazine.

"This was possible only because the railroads themselves had become marketing-minded. 'Ten years ago,' says James Cathcart, Pullman's director of long-range planning, 'we wouldn't have dared talk to the railroads' customers.' But in 1961, when Jack E. Gilliland of the St. Louis–San Francisco Railroad came to Pullman with the idea for an auto rack car, Pullman already had men in Detroit working with the automobile companies. The eventual result was that Pullman played a large role in winning back to the railroads 50 percent of all autos hauled."[27]

During World War II, the plant in Butler, Pennsylvania, produced more than 7 million artillery shells. (*Photo courtesy of Butler County Historical Society.*)

Pullman continued to beef up its research and development in the making of freight cars as well. *Forbes* wrote that the auto rack car would not have been possible without the company's development of the cushion underframe, which prevented damage to the autos.[28]

Railroads also had become more attentive to shippers' needs and began offering an increasingly wider variety of specialty cars. But because railcar leasing companies and manufacturers could often build specialized cars cheaper than the railroads could themselves, some railroads stopped building their own cars. Railcar companies began designing specialty cars that included boxcars up to 85 feet long with triple the capacity of the old 40-foot models; tri-level automobile carriers; large, covered hoppers; pressurized dry-bulk carriers; and jumbo tank cars.[29]

When Pullman Standard introduced the covered hopper car in 1966, the innovation shook the industry. Traditionally, grain was shipped in boxcars, which tied up labor and time, but with the covered hopper car, loading and unloading were vastly speeded up because the car could be loaded from the top and unloaded through the bottom. Despite the obvious advantages, Pullman had to persuade the management of Santa Fe Railroad to give covered hopper grain cars a try, according to a 1966 article in *Forbes* magazine.

"The result was the largest order in railroad-car building history, 2,500 covered hoppers to be built at Pullman's Butler, Pennsylvania, plant. That plant, which used to make each of five lines of cars, has been expanded and changed to produce only covered hoppers and flatcars, but at the rate of 60 a day vs. the former 47 a day. Furthermore, for the first time in many years, the assembly line is running on three shifts."[30]

Pullman employee Don Bodinger, who worked for the company in 1966, recalled the frenetic pace in a 1999 interview. "We were building so many cars a day every day for years and years for trailer and container haulings," he said.[31]

At its peak, Pullman Standard held 25 percent of the industry's total production. Led by former astronaut General James McDivitt, Pullman raked

in huge profits, topping $50 million on sales of around $800 million.

Pulling Out and Shutting Down

But the company had mistakenly stayed within the narrow niche of boxcars and hopper cars, even as new concepts like intermodal containers began to take hold. Furthermore, the company had grown sluggish and was hampered by its relations with its unions. Its competitors were more nimble and could quickly respond to a customer's requests. Pullman Standard, in the words of the late George Green, a former Pullman president and an outspoken stockholder, had the attitude of "the hell with you. You're stupid. Take what we give or else."[32]

Throughout the seventies, Pullman found itself in nightmare after contractual nightmare. In 1972, for instance, the company had won a $210 million contract to build 745 subway cars for the New York City transit system. At $282,000 apiece, this was the largest subway car order in New York's history. But Pullman Standard badly miscalculated how much it would actually cost to build the cars.

"The magnitude of the losses facing Pullman can be gauged by current prices," noted an article in *Business Week*. "The most recent order for self-propelled electric passenger cars in the U.S. was placed last month with General Electric Company at a price of $730,000 per car. The order was for railroad commuter cars rather than subway cars, but that in itself does not account for the price difference. Nor does inflation wholly account for it. Pullman obtained the New York City order — the biggest ever placed — by shaving its cost estimates to the lowest possible point."[33]

Pullman lost $46 million on that contract, and that same year the company got an order from Amtrak for 284 bi-level cars, called Superliners, to operate initially over routes west of Chicago and New Orleans at a cost of $848,000 each. Pullman did better on this contract. It at least broke even.[34]

Pullman's chief executive, Samuel B. Casey, finally announced in March 1979 that the company would stop making passenger cars and concentrate on its profitable freight car and

Pullman Standard built 745 subway cars for New York City, the largest such contract in the city's history up to that time.

truck trailer businesses. Although its fame was founded on passenger cars, the business had become an insufferable headache for Pullman's executives. "It's a lousy market, and we're getting out," Casey said. "We've been going in that direction since 1972."[35] Pullman was the fourth American company in the 1970s to abandon the passenger car business. Only the Budd Company in Philadelphia, busy with rapid transit cars and electric locomotive shells, remained.[36]

In 1980, Wheelabrator-Frye, a New Hampshire-based conglomerate, bought Pullman Inc. in a highly publicized $600 million takeover. The jewel in the buy was not Pullman's freight-car building business, however. It was M.W. Kellogg, the company's engineering division, which Pullman had acquired in 1944.[37] Don Bodinger, a longtime Pullman employee, recalled that "Wheelabrator didn't want anything to do with freight cars.... We weren't sure what was going to happen."[38]

What did happen was the closing of the famous Bessemer and Butler plants. Bessemer was the first. Workers shut down the lines that had built more than 1 million cars.[39] This scene was replayed in Butler and the other plants, and more than 5,000 workers joined the exodus streaming from railcar assembly lines.

With the railcar business on the skids, Wheelabrator reorganized the Pullman division into Pullman Transportation (a holding company with Pullman Leasing and Pullman Standard) and spun it off.[40]

A year and a half later, Trinity purchased Pullman Standard. Trinity's cost for the acquisition did not stop with the purchase price, however. Pullman's assembly lines were equipped with outmoded equipment and manned by the ghosts of its past. They required expensive overhauling to prepare for the return of happy days to the railcar industry that those in the business knew had to be coming. As Ray Wallace later noted, "We needed the ability to survive time. Unfortunately, I didn't realize it was going to take as long as it did."[41]

When the railcar market cratered, Trinity's other product lines, like this oilfield pump jack, took up the slack.

CHAPTER TEN

THE GATHERING

*"Past investment of management talent, capital and other resources
has helped solidify Trinity's position as a leader in the market it serves."*

— Ray Wallace, 1989[1]

S HORTLY AFTER TRINITY acquired Pullman Standard in 1984, Tim Wallace toured the company's cavernous Bessemer plant. Empty and dark, the plant echoed with the wind that beat on the side of the building, Wallace recalled, giving the facility an eerie feeling. Work had been left as if employees had gone home on Friday and expected to return on Monday. "It was like a time warp," he said.[2]

The purchase of Pullman Standard was actually the second of six railcar-related acquisitions Trinity completed in the eighties. By the end of the decade, when the market for railcars finally rebounded, Trinity had gathered together a remarkable team of companies and engineering talent.

Just as significant as the acquisitions, however, was the opportunity presented by General American Transportation Corporation, the nation's largest railcar leasing company. In late 1983, General American (the railcar subsidiary of GATX) had decided to outsource the manufacture of its railcars to concentrate on engineering, service and leasing operations. GATX sought a manufacturer with the breadth of abilities to meet its needs. The company came to the conclusion that Trinity was the right manufacturer for the job.

The GATX Deal

When General American Transportation Corporation announced it was getting out of

railcar manufacturing, analysts applauded the decision. With its 55,000 railcars, its leasing business made a lot more financial sense in an industry where overcapacity was a continuing problem.

Arriving at the decision was not easy, however. GATX had been building railcars since 1902, when it was incorporated as the German-American Car Company. The company was founded in 1898 by a former Chicago stockyard worker named Max Epstein. Epstein originated the idea of leasing specialty cars to shippers on a long-term basis instead of renting out railcars as needed, which was the common practice.[3] Since then, the company built, sold and leased its own railcars.

After the railcar industry foundered, a debate raged among senior management and the board of directors about whether to get out of manufacturing altogether to concentrate on leasing, which does not entail the high overhead costs that come with production lines. In the end, the recession was expected to last at least until 1990, which was far too long to wait. That's when GATX turned to Trinity for its railcars.[4] "They were very good builders," said Ward Fuller, who at the time was GATX's vice president in charge of finance and

A wood-chip rotary dump gondola made by Trinity. The company's engineering ability grew exponentially in the 1980s.

Tim Wallace, third from left, with representatives from GATX and Olin Chemicals. At the time this photo was taken in 1987, Trinity had reached the halfway point in the delivery of 200 caustic soda tank cars to Olin.

would become president in 1991. "As Ray Wallace likes to say, they know how to bend steel, weld it and join it together."[5]

James Goff, who was then president of GATX, commented in April 1984 that "our announced strategy has been to concentrate our resources on railcar engineering and leasing, while leaving manufacturing to others with newer production facilities. Trinity's modern plants and technology make it the perfect manufacturing partner."[6]

Under the contract, Trinity would build railcars developed with GATX engineering. The work included GATX-designed tank cars that were lighter and more efficient, as well as GATX's proprietary Airslide and TankTrain system cars. The Airslide car was a specialty covered hopper for transporting flour, sugar, starch and other items. The TankTrain system involved a series of interconnecting cars for carrying high-volume liquids. Under the system, a string of cars could be filled or emptied from a single hook-up point. Both GATX and Trinity would offer the new cars to customers for lease or sale. Trinity also would make repair parts for new tank cars and for existing cars in the GATX fleet.

The decision was a courageous one for GATX. "They were one of the first companies to make a strategic decision to outsource and focus on their core competency of leasing," noted Tim Wallace in 1999.[7]

Ray Wallace saw incredible potential in the partnership. "By entering into this contract with GATX, we can extend our manufacturing and engineering capabilities to work with the country's largest tank car lessor on new tank cars and proprietary designs for specialty cars," he said in an April 1984 news release. "We will also be able to increase the variety of cars we currently offer our other customers."[8]

In spite of Trinity's capabilities — or because of them — GATX was not as thrilled, and the relationship did not go smoothly at first. "It created a lot of controversy," Tim Wallace recalled. "It was hard to get to where we were dancing on the same dance floor."[9] Several years would pass, but the relationship eventually deepened between Trinity and GATX. (See sidebar on page 106.)

Tank Lining and Repair

A similar relations problem confronted Tim Wallace, who had to weld a host of once-competing railcar firms into a cohesive railcar group. Engineering-wise, Trinity would possess the most formidable presence in the industry. Getting them to work together, however, was the problem. When the consolidation began, Ray Wallace told his son, "This is going to be one heck of a good learning experience for you."[10]

Trinity's consolidation of the railcar industry began in February 1984 with the purchase of Tank Lining Corporation from its owner and cofounder, Wally Cathcart. Located in Oakdale, just outside Pittsburgh, Pennsylvania, the 34-year-old company was one of the largest and best-known firms specializing in lining tanks with protective coating. Tank linings protect a tank from the material the tank carries and also protect the material from the tank. With everything from corn syrup to hydrochloric acid transported in tank cars, the linings are custom-made in strict adherence to increasingly stringent environmental standards. Tank lining was one of those disciplines that many railcar builders believed was best to outsource because linings required a particular brand of expertise.

At its peak, Tank Lining had grown to a respectable $9 million just prior to the collapse of the rail market. Cathcart had expanded his operations by adding shops in Texas and Illinois. He lined about 15 cars a day, and almost all of his business involved lining new cars. "We had all these production lines set up, so when the halt [in the railcar market] came, we were without customers," Cathcart recalled. He said his sales-people did a fantastic job of branching out, and the company returned to almost 70 percent of what it had been in dollar volume, but he remained just barely profitable.[11]

Cathcart, approaching 60 years of age, said he had decided it was time to retire. Tank Lining Corporation had come to Trinity's attention because it was the only such company with the ability to line large-diameter tanks in the field with coating that had to be baked at 400 degrees Fahrenheit. When Trinity heard Cathcart wanted to sell, the company studied the operation and gave Cathcart a call. "They said they were thinking of a price in the ball park of ... well, they named a figure that was in a ballpark that I was just delighted to play in," said Cathcart.[12]

The same year as the Tank Lining purchase, Trinity bought almost all the assets of Quick Car of Saginaw, Texas, from Halliburton Company. Quick Car had been finishing cars for Trinity since 1976 by putting wheels, paint and other necessities on cars manufactured at other Trinity plants. The acquisition of this Saginaw plant marked an important point in Trinity's history because it was Trinity's first railcar repair shop.[13] Combining Quick Car with the earlier acquisition, Trinity formed the Tank Lining Railcar Repair Division.

Strengthening the Core

Trinity added more rail-related companies, notably Greenville Steel Car Company of Greenville, Pennsylvania, and Standard Forgings of Chicago (both in 1986); Ortner Freight Car of Mt. Orab, Ohio (1987); and Lone Star Railcar of Saginaw, Texas

(1989). Like many of Trinity's acquisitions, each had a rich history of accomplishments.

Greenville Steel Car Company, for instance, had been in business since 1918 and at its height had grown to more than $280 million in revenue — second only to Pullman Standard. Keith Hittle, former president of Greenville, explained that Greenville had built the first all-steel freight cars, departing from the traditional use of wood.

Greenville had been owned by Pittsburgh Forgings since 1932 but was sold to Amco Pittsburgh in 1979. After the railcar crash, Greenville stayed viable through its small lease fleet of about 3,000 cars. "We had decent cash flow," Hittle recalled. "Then Amco sold our lease fleet. After that, it wasn't too hard to figure out what was next. They put us on the auction block."[14]

The next company purchased was Standard Forgings, which made railcar axles. Helmut Hvizdalek, who ran Standard Forgings as general manager and co-owner, had been watching Trinity gradually overtake the famous names he had been dealing with for years. Eventually, Ray Wallace approached the owners of the struggling Standard Forgings with an attractive offer. "We could see over the years that this was a very aggressive and very strong company," Hvizdalek said. "As they became stronger, they wanted to be more self-sufficient."[15]

Before it began making railcars in 1918, Greenville Steel Car had been a stamping plant and supplied fenders and other parts to the Empire Automobile Company. Below is a restored 1913 "Little Aristocrat," owned by Greenville and then sold to the local historical society. (*Photo courtesy of the Greenville Historical Society.*)

104   THE LEGEND OF TRINITY INDUSTRIES

The acquisition lessened Trinity's dependence on outside suppliers for axles and other critical railcar components. When it first entered the railcar market, securing supplies of these items had been a major problem because the industry giants swallowed up supplies as fast as Standard could manufacture components.

Hvizdalek was asked to stay on as head of the wholly owned subsidiary, which has grown to become one of the largest builders of railcar axles in the world. (Over time Trinity added other axle makers. In 1999, the subsidiary was producing about 180,000 axles a year.)[16]

The purchase of Ortner Freight Car brought to Trinity the design expertise behind the development of the rapid discharge car. Ortner was founded in 1953 in Covington, Kentucky, with 12 employees repairing and scrapping old railcars. It first began to build completed cars in 1958 for the U.S. Army. In 1961 the company made a name for itself with the rapid discharge car, an innovation that unloaded a car completely within 30 minutes. Operations eventually expanded to Mt. Orab, Ohio, which became Ortner's new home in 1981 when the Covington plant was closed down. (Ortner by then was owned by Avondale

Industries, a joint venture between Ogden Corporation, Ortner's parent company since 1969, and Avondale Shipyards.)

"You know, we had a world of wealth of engineering knowledge that came from all these different companies and different disciplines, so believe me, there were some troubling times trying to marry all these groups together," remarked Trinity Vice President Wayne Hacker, who began working for Ortner as soon as he graduated from high school in 1967.[17]

Learning New Ropes

Tim Wallace soon had his hands full. After he brought the Bessemer plant on line, he was sent to manage Standard Forgings. Wallace said he had to learn the business of axle manufacturing from the ground up. Complicating his education was a series of axle failures, one of which caused a derailment.

The original site of Ortner Freight Car, in Covington, Kentucky. This photo was taken in 1956. Operations expanded to Mt. Orab, Ohio, which became Ortner's new headquarters in 1981.

The first Rapid Discharge Car was introduced in 1961. This car was Ortner's 10,000th RD1, as they were known.

The axles had been built prior to Trinity's acquisition. Standard Forgings had been beset with disappearing orders and had cut back on its ultrasonic testing program. Investigating the problem, Wallace and Hvizdalek discovered the axle had not been tested as extensively as it should have been. "I had to get a quick education," Wallace recalled. "I was called up to Washington in front of the American Association of Railroads. About 20 people were in the room asking me, 'Okay, you're running this company. What the hell are you doing?'"[18]

Wallace and Hvizdalek immediately began putting together a massive testing program to examine all of the axles Standard Forgings had produced within the previous two years. "We pulled all the axles, and I had to understand the forging process, the ultrasonic testing, the chemicals and the physicals associated with axles, and all the levels of testing," said Wallace. "It was a great experience for me, working under a crisis of learning how to put a team together and make something happen."[19]

Similar incidents cropped up with the Ortner and Greenville acquisitions. Some operators experienced problems with cars they bought before Trinity acquired the companies. Legally, Trinity was not responsible for the past sins of its acquisitions. Tim Wallace and Bill Neewby, who was vice president in charge of sales and marketing at that time, talked over the situation and decided to make good on the customers' issues. "We stepped up to the bar and helped those people resolve their problems, at Trinity's cost," noted Neewby.

"That helped build the organization and our relationships. The society that buys railcars is very close knit. If you have one unhappy customer, everybody in the industry is aware of it, sometimes even before you are. Well, Ray Wallace backed the both of us, and I think that was a vital part in making us the company we are today in the freight car part of the market."[20]

A GENTLEMAN'S BET

WHEN WARD FULLER BECAME PRESident of General American, the railcar leasing subsidiary of GATX, he joked that he couldn't use the "T" word — that is, Trinity — in the office. Fuller was appointed president of the subsidiary in 1991, about seven years after GATX had agreed to outsource its railcars to Trinity. Though outsourcing was a wise business decision, it nevertheless did not sit well with GATX's management. "The feeling among senior management at the time was that this was the beginning of the end," Fuller said in an interview. "They felt that Trinity would build its lease fleet while ours declined. When I got here in 1991, there were a lot of long faces, and in fact our fleet had been declining."[1]

One of Fuller's first actions as president was to meet with Trinity's senior staff to work out a mutually beneficial strategic plan. Fuller said he could see that leasing was in fact a secondary activity for Trinity, one used to help support its manufacturing operations. The meeting was an immediate success, Fuller recalled.

"I liked both Ray and Tim right off the bat. It was clear to me in talking with them that their love was manufacturing. When I told them that we were going to reinvigorate General American and create a new strategic plan, I would say that there was no one happier than Ray and Tim Wallace for us to get out there and become a leader in that industry, and have both our market shares grow."[2]

This was the beginning of a strategic partnership. Both sides saw an opportunity to forge a unique relationship that went beyond normal business dealings. "We were able to develop a lot of flexibility in terms of manufacturing, every bit as much as if we had our own manufacturing operations," said Fuller.[3]

The key to the relationship was trust, the strength of which was illustrated when Fuller made a bet with Ray Wallace that General American would capture a certain percentage of the market. If General American crossed that threshold, Wallace would take his wife on a covered wagon ride, something she had always wanted to do but that he hadn't.

Not long afterwards, Wallace granted Fuller the use of his spacious ranch for an Outward Bound–type of weekend for Fuller's employees. Fuller said he planned a four-hour hike for about 90 of his employees. When they reached a bunkhouse, a number of Trinity's executive staff would be on hand. Together they would throw a party — or so Wallace believed. "Ray thought it would be sort of fun to bring people from our companies together and that it would be a good way to bring our leadership together as well," Fuller said.

Unknown at this time to Wallace, Fuller had won the bet. "So Ray's looking at his watch, expecting us to arrive, when everyone heard the click, click, click," Fuller said. "Instead of seeing people, the first thing he sees are horses and a covered wagon. From the bunkhouse, you see five covered wagons pull up with a ton of people and a bunch of horses. We've got a big Trinity/General American logo on the side of one of the wagons. I got up and said, 'I think it's time for this Texas gentleman to fulfill his obligations.'"[4]

Wallace and his wife got on the covered wagon and traveled to the site of the party. "That was a special day for our organizations," concluded Fuller. "I would say that was the day we put aside the barriers of traditional perceptions of customer and supplier and really began to work together as one."[5]

The Beginnings of Trouble

In 1984, as Trinity was moving into the dominant position in the railcar industry, the corporate offices moved into new quarters. Since 1957, the headquarters had been located at 4001 Irving Boulevard. Now, beginning in June, corporate officers reported for work at a gleaming white 10-story building located at 2525 Stemmons Freeway, northwest of downtown Dallas. The 113,600-square-foot building was fully occupied that November.[21]

As they settled into their new surroundings, Trinity's executives had the unpleasant task of recording the company's first loss in 27 years — $6 million on revenues of $455 million. Demand for new railcars for the nation's fleet had increased but was still at a lower level than annual retirements. In short, more cars were going out of service than were being replaced. This would eventually mushroom into a full-blown transportation crisis similar to the one experienced in the seventies.

Ken Lewis, who worked with CFO Ed Breeding, said he remembered that the board of directors had the difficult decision of whether to pay a dividend each quarter. They decided to continue the dividends.

At the heart of the problem was a regulatory dispute between shippers and railroads. Under the rules set forth by the Interstate Commerce Commission, railroads had the right to exclude from their tracks all shipper-owned cars. They invoked that right following the rush of orders in the early 1980s, forcing shippers, which owned two-fifths of the national fleet, to rely on railroad-owned cars.[22] The practice discouraged replacement orders that normally would have been placed by shippers as their cars became obsolete.

This dispute was eventually resolved but not before the number of railcar manufacturers plummeted from 17 to 6. By the mid-eighties, Trinity controlled more than half the industry's entire output capacity.[23]

All five business segments — railcars, containers, structural products, marine products and metal components — suffered losses during this period, especially in the shipbuilding units. Nationwide, shipbuilders were in dire straits. One hundred and ten shipyards had closed down in the first half of the eighties, and more closings were anticipated. The oil industry was still flat because low demand and oversupply had idled thousands of offshore drilling rigs. Federal subsidies for commercial ships were lacking when American shipbuilders faced increased overseas competition. In the fifties American shipbuilders built most of the world's fleets. By the 1980s, three-quarters of the world's ships came out of Korean and Japanese shipyards, where labor costs were less and government subsidies were common. In a 1985 report, the International Trade Commission said that "South Korea and Japan can build the same commercial ship twice as fast as any American shipyard at half the cost."[24]

To cope with the downturn, Trinity cut costs and jobs and rid itself of nonessential plants and equipment in its marine products segment. The company also pursued military orders with renewed vigor, viewing them as a way to bridge the slump in the offshore drilling business.[25] The efforts showed some reward when the U.S. Navy awarded an $85 million contract to Halter Marine to build six ocean surveillance ships. The 224-foot

Trinity Industries' new corporate headquarters, located at 2525 Stemmons Freeway.

ships, known as T-AGOS, were used for antisubmarine warfare.[26]

In addition, Bell Halter, the joint venture between Halter Marine and Bell Aerospace Textron, had won two Navy shipbuilding and design contracts totaling $31 million for engines, clutches and other equipment to be used in five air-cushion landing craft that Bell Halter was to build. The joint venture also embarked on rebuilding the U.S. Navy's minesweeping fleet, which had dwindled dangerously from a high of 300 during World War II to just three active vessels and 18 naval reserve craft.[27]

The steel products segment showed the best performance, which meant it lost the least money. After completing a number of utility plants in the early 1980s, Trinity caught the wave of a boom in high-rise office construction. Such work was fueled by a need for more space, as well as by foreign investment, inflation-indexed mortgages and equity participation by lenders.

Mosher provided 24,000 tons of structural steel for Houston's Transco Tower, which was completed in 1983. It was "dubbed the nation's largest building outside a downtown area. Uncrowded by other skyscrapers, it can be seen for miles away," noted an article in the *Houston Chronicle*. "The revolving beacon on top is a nighttime landmark, especially for confused motorists lost on the city's southwest side."[28] The 64-story building, reminiscent of the Art Deco towers from the 1920s, was renamed the Williams Tower in 1999.

An oversupply of office space in Houston and other Southwestern cities shifted most big-building construction work to the Northeast and Midwest. Mosher was providing steel for the huge red, white and blue George R. Brown Convention Center in Houston but subcontracted with a Korean company to supply specialized large columns for the $105 million building. In a fiercely competitive market, John T. Sanford, a Trinity vice president, said, "Had we bid it ourselves, we wouldn't have been competitive." He noted that Trinity was taking work that was marginally profitable, or break-even, just to keep its plants operating in the depressed market.[29] Still, Mosher had enough large jobs to keep its three Texas plants running at close to capacity.

There was one bright spot in 1985 when Mosher was inducted into the Centennial Circle, a group of firms honored annually by the Dallas County Heritage Society at the celebration of their 100th anniversaries. Two others were inducted that year along with Mosher: *The Dallas Morning News* and Dr Pepper, the soft drink giant that began in Waco and moved to Dallas in 1923.

The rough conditions extended to Trinity's original product line, liquefied petroleum gas containers, which felt the effects of an abundance of natural gas supplies. Utility companies began extending natural gas lines to more communities, reducing the need for storage tanks. Likewise, sales of anhydrous ammonia fertilizer containers were down because of the depressed farm economy.

In early 1986, Trinity closed its Lincoln, Nebraska, plant because of the poor farm economy. The Nebraska plant had operated for 25 years and at the time of the closing had two dozen employees. "The downturn in the farm economy hit us hard," Trinity executive Lee McElroy said at the time. "Farming has become a different ball game. We feel that the trend is to see the individual farmer replaced by corporate farming."[30]

With an oil glut forcing down prices, the market for offshore supply boats dried up. Shown here is a 150-foot tug at its launch, one of the few orders in the mid-1980s.

Bridging the Gap

Just as it had done with the railcar business, Trinity used the downturn in the early 1980s to buy steel fabricators with the anticipation that bridge work would return. Trinity snapped up the assets of other companies, including Allied Structural Steel Company, one of the premier steel fabricators in the country, which was even older than Mosher. Based in Chicago Heights, Illinois, the company had largely shut down from lack of work when Trinity purchased it.

Allied had a long history of steel fabrication, providing steel for buildings, power plants and bridges for many years. The company traced its Iowa beginnings to the Union Iron Works, formed in 1868, and grew out of the affiliation of a number of companies in 1941. The Union Iron Works — consisting of a brick machine shop with an adjacent foundry, boiler and blacksmith shops — later was taken over by the younger Clinton Bridge Company.

Before Trinity purchased it, Allied's projects included steel for the first 22 stories of the towering 100-story John Hancock Center in Chicago and 4,000 tons of steel for the Perrine Bridge over the Snake River in Twin Falls, Idaho. It also had supplied steel for nuclear power plants in Arizona and in Richland, Washington, and furnished over 4,000 tons of structural steel items for what was known as the Moonport in Cape Canaveral, Florida.[31]

Trinity also acquired Anderson "Safeway" Guardrail Corporation in Ohio and, several years later, Kentucky Galvanizing Inc., in Elizabethtown, another guardrail maker, which added key management and increased Trinity's customer base and market.[32]

Other lines were added to its structural products segment to help fill any gaps in production schedules because of changing economic conditions. These included pump jacks for oil well completions and the truck trailers, or chassis, upon which shipping containers are mounted. Trinity manufactured the pump jacks — the constantly moving up-and-down arm seen at producing wells — for two large national suppliers as well as for direct sale to other customers.[33]

Meanwhile, Trinity had worked hard to expand its marketing area and production capacity in its metal components segment and had achieved much success. It had installed fittings and forging equipment from the Babcock & Wilcox facility in West Memphis and the large hot-forming head machine in Navasota, Texas.

In addition to its other segments, Trinity now had become the largest low-cost manufacturer of weld fittings, flanges and container heads.[34] These items were used in piping systems and on pressure and non-pressure tank containers for the oil and gas industry. A business history publication noted that "Trinity remained the American leader in this highly active market."[35]

Trinity introduced chassis as a new product. Along with pump jacks, fittings and flanges, the chassis line kept Trinity busy during the downturn.

Toward the end of the decade, many of Trinity's markets had begun to turn around, just as Ray Wallace knew they would. In 1989, Trinity hit the $1 billion mark for the first time, with the Railcar Division leading the way. Net income had hit $30.3 million. "We knew that railcars was not a business that would be gone forever," Wallace was quoted as saying in a *Forbes* article. "We also knew you didn't often get opportunities to acquire large portions of the industry at reasonable prices."[36]

In his letter to shareholders, Wallace noted that the "past investment of management talent, capital and other resources has helped solidify Trinity's position as a leader in the market it serves.... Business prospects are continuing to improve."[37]

But in an interview a decade later, Wallace downplayed the event. "[Hitting the $1 billion mark] was great," he said, "but our earnings weren't as proportionately large as we would have liked. All this did was just encourage us to go on to the next benchmark, which I thought was pretty far off. Fortunately, it didn't take that long."[38]

The Birth of QuEST

Trinity was still confronted with the problem of pulling the people from its many acquisitions together so business units could function as a team. In taking over the Railcar Division, Tim Wallace was responsible for melding the many cultures together. He knew he faced a formidable task. "We had a hodgepodge of car designs. We had a hodgepodge of cultures and people," he said. "In the late eighties I struggled with pulling this group together to where we were under the same umbrella. But we were never a company big on signing up for some program."[39]

At this time, the concept of TQM — Total Quality Management — was in vogue. It moved like a wave, radiating to and from connected industries. "It moved through the automobile industry, and because automobiles have a lot of plastic in them, it moved to the plastics industry. Since plastics are carried on railcars, it moved into the railcar industry," Tim Wallace explained.[40]

Wallace hired two consultants, Roger Beynon and Henry Rosen, to help him devise a program centered on training and continuous improvement. Beynon helped Wallace develop training and communication modules, while Rosen, an advertising consultant, assisted with packaging the program, which they called QuEST — an acronym for Quality, Efficiency, Safety and Training. ("Training" was eventually replaced by the word "Trust" in the acronym because training was seen as a component of trust.)

QuEST was a clear departure from Trinity's traditional command-and-control structure, which worked fine when it came to repetitive designs. But the designs coming out of GATX were becoming less repetitive, and the whole quality movement said no, don't shove your standard car down your customer's throat. "We were transitioning from 'let's go copy a design and beat them on the field' to 'let's listen to the customers, understand what their needs are, and design a car centered around those needs,'" said Wallace.

"That was a scary thought to a high volume, repetitive manufacturer. GATX would give us an order for 100 cars, we'd build them, then all of a sudden they would change the next design. My people came to me complaining about how they kept changing their designs. I had to change our mindset. I said we shouldn't get uptight about GATX changing their designs; we should instead become quick-change artists ourselves. If we could figure out how to adapt to their change more quickly, then they could sell or lease more cars."[41]

This meant getting out to customers to learn where their bottlenecks and troublespots were occurring. Wallace assembled teams to work with customers such as GATX, Cargill and Archer-Daniels-Midland. It wasn't long before the value of this type of relationship became apparent.

The surge of replacement orders had begun, and Trinity was transforming itself into an innovative designer. As the last decade of the millennium began, the management change that began under Tim Wallace in the Railcar Division would take hold and gradually spread throughout the company. "The traditional philosophy built one heck of a good company," Tim Wallace said. "But we got to the point where if we were going to grow at the pace we needed to, I had to start empowering people and letting them take some ownership."[42]

Highway construction boomed throughout the 1990s, helping to push Trinity's revenues to new records.

CHAPTER ELEVEN

BREAKING NEW RECORDS

"If you're in a replacement business, you just have to let time work for you. We've always lined up with the contrarians."

— Ray Wallace, quoted in *Forbes* magazine, 1994[1]

IN THE NINETIES, THE RAILCAR market returned with a vengeance. By the middle of the decade, Trinity's railcar segment became a billion-dollar business by itself, and the company surpassed the $2 billion mark, reaching $2.3 billion in revenue. This milestone occurred just six years after the company passed the $1 billion benchmark.

"We work better because our people have been here a long time and are looking long term," Ray Wallace told a reporter from *The Dallas Morning News*.[2] The board of directors and the financial community understood that Trinity was a company whose growth would be long term.[3]

Wallace no longer spent a great deal of time on day-to-day business operations. "When I was 65, we had too much that needed to be done and young people who needed seasoning," he commented. The passage of time, as well as the recent trials the company surmounted, provided the seasoning, and Wallace felt that his younger management was ready to begin taking over. "All the people running our major product lines are in their forties. They really could survive quite well without us oldsters."[4]

Tim Wallace was a key part of the management team. He was asked to join the board in 1992, an opportunity that quickly gave him a wider perspective. "I've always tried to jump perspectives, from ours to our customers, suppliers and so on," he said. "I was able to move to the board and jump to a director's perspective, which gave me a whole new depth of understanding of what is involved in running a public company."[5]

Still president and chief operating officer of the railcar group, Tim Wallace would soon witness the reward for the company's careful preparation and patient waiting. Thousands of obsolete cars had fallen out of service without replacement, and the situation had almost reached a crisis point. Agricultural and transportation experts worried that grain might be left to rot in bulging silos for want of railcars, the same situation that faced the nation back in the seventies.[6]

In April 1990, Trinity purchased Beaird Industries, a $66 million conglomerate that helped boost Trinity's growing container business in the early nineties. Beaird's 650 employees made huge custom vessels, desalinators, heat exchangers and other specialized metal products. Under its trademark, Maxim, Beaird made silencers that cut down noise in piston and turbine engines. Its desalinators provided fresh water for offshore platforms, nuclear submarines, yachts, luxury liners and other naval vessels.[7]

A Trinity-made LPG underground storage tank, which could hold 30,000 gallons, on its way to the museum and welcome center at Mount Rushmore.

For Trinity, the year 1990 was outstanding in terms of revenue and profit. Revenue climbed 57 percent — comprising half of Trinity's total $1.3 billion that year. Operating profit increased by 35 percent, reaching $55 million. But that was only the start of an extraordinary decade of prosperity and creativity.

Working Together

The company's engineers entered the decade with the willingness and backing to experiment. New designs and concepts, some successful and others not, began flowing from the teams Tim Wallace and Steve Smith, vice president of engineering, had established.

The first major innovation of the decade was the SMART car. Unveiled in May 1990 at the Intermodal Expo, SMART (an acronym for Secured Modular Automotive Rail Transport) was built for Union Pacific Railroad.[8] A two-unit fully enclosed articulated spine car with aerodynamic skirting and automobile-carrying modules, the car could be stacked two or three high, depending on the vehicles carried. The railcar, according to *Railway Age*, was "evolutionary because it's designed to mate with existing autorack cars and revolutionary because it's designed to do a better and more cost-effective job of moving motor vehicles."[9]

Unfortunately, the concept was not successful because of its cost and because the autorack car-carrying system, which had been in place for years, was too firmly entrenched. Car dealerships and railroads were not willing to invest in the necessary infrastructure.

Although not a commercial success, the SMART car was in fact a triumph of Trinity's engineering and design ability. The design was an unmistakable mark of innovation. It demonstrated that Trinity's engineers had the courage and the backing to strike out in new directions by working closely with customers. Improved designs began to stream from Trinity's engineering and design teams, and ongoing improvements were instituted by Tim Wallace, by then chief operating officer and president of the Railcar Division. QuEST was helping Trinity to reap both new orders and industry-wide recognition.

Steve Smith was given the responsibility of getting all of the different engineering teams to work from a common set of procedures. "They all had their own drawing systems, their own way of doing things down to the name of their company on the designs," explained Smith.

"We had kept the names of Pullman Standard, Greenville and the others because of their reputations. They were still semi-independent, so we created a bunch of teams with each of the individual engineering groups to develop a common number system, a common drawing system, etc."[10]

With Trinity's own reputation now an asset, the individual company names were not as important. Developing common procedures sped

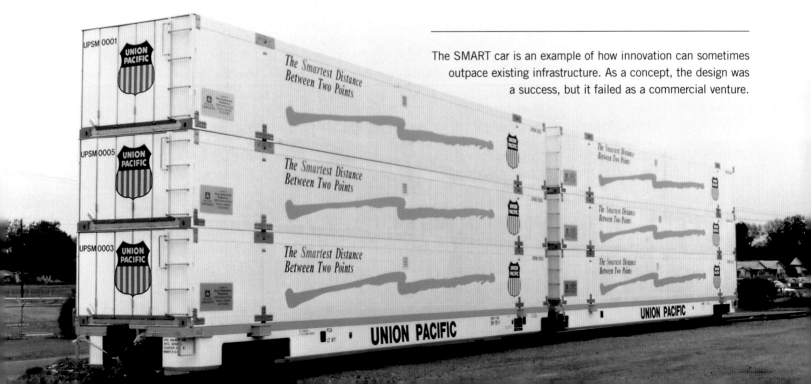

The SMART car is an example of how innovation can sometimes outpace existing infrastructure. As a concept, the design was a success, but it failed as a commercial venture.

In 1991, Staley Manufacturing presented Ray Wallace with a "Transportation Supplier of the Year" award for Trinity's on-time, on-spec delivery of a variety of railcars.

approval times by the American Association of Railroads, the industry's governing body.

In 1991, Trinity teamed up with Texas Eastman to produce 60 tank cars to the customer's specifications. Texas Eastman would then lease the cars from Trinity's Leasing Division. Texas Eastman, based in Longview, a unit of Eastman Kodak's Eastman Chemical Company, operated a 2,100-car fleet, which included both hopper and tank cars. "We're pleased that the best manufacturer we could select for this order happened to be located right here in Longview," Texas Eastman spokesman Jack Goodwyn said. "While working with Trinity locally will be convenient, Trinity was selected for reasons other than geographic proximity. We believe they share the same commitment to quality that Texas Eastman is known for."[11]

Charlie Eller, customer service representative for Trinity's Longview plant, described Trinity and Texas Eastman as a perfect match. He noted that both companies focused on quality enhancement efforts, with Trinity's being QuEST and Texas Eastman's commitment to the Quality Management Process. "Both companies have the same philosophy of employee involvement and empowerment," Eller said. "And we both

believe strongly that the key to success is a close working partnership."[12]

This close working partnership could be seen at a pre-production meeting in December 1990 at Trinity's Longview East plant. Texas Eastman executives reviewed blueprints and procedures and then took a walking tour. At various work stations, the employees who would manufacture the cars discussed their work, including key processes and improvements.

Tailoring a car's design and its speed of manufacturing was key in getting an order from A.E. Staley Manufacturing Company, one of the largest producers of corn sweeteners in the United States. In 1990, Staley needed its specialty tank cars designed and delivered within a year. The car had to adhere to a lengthy list of specifications, in terms of both design and financing, noted Richard Brown, executive vice president of Trinity Industries Leasing.

"These tank cars use a lot of stainless steel and have an interior food-grade lining to protect the product. The cars are being used primarily to carry high-fructose corn syrup. It's an extremely high-quality product that requires a very clean, sanitary, high-quality car."[13]

The car was completed within the time frame, and Trinity went on to produce 523 more cars of varying types for Staley. In 1991, Staley presented Trinity with a "Transportation Supplier of the Year" award for its on-time, on-spec delivery. "We presented the award because, of that entire order, only six or eight cars needed very minor corrections, which were completed before delivery," noted Patrick Murphy, Staley's director of transportation.[14] Later, Dow Chemical Company's transportation segment awarded Trinity a certificate as a "Qualified Supplier" based on a quality standards program Dow had begun in 1990. Dow had been pleased with Trinity, whose QuEST program "fit neatly with Dow's objectives" and high standards for its suppliers.[15]

As a company-wide program, QuEST was maturing. Trinity's workers were organized into "Natural Work Groups" and "Cross-Functional Teams" to tackle individual orders. They discussed the customer's schedule and design needs, the impact on other schedules and potential problem areas, as well as tooling and material issues, to make sure the necessary pieces were in place before they even started on an order. An article in the trade magazine *Progressive Railroading* described the process.

"Before any torch, bolt, rivet or electrode touches steel, the car is completely dissected to see how it and the manufacturing process can meet the customer's needs. The teams in essence 'buy in' to the production of the car. If the customer has a short lead time on the car, the Trinity teams prepare a plan of action on how they can meet that schedule. If they need to work X hours of overtime or add extra people to their shift, they come back to management and tell them what is required and make recommendations."[16]

"With QuEST, every employee knows that we want to operate under what we call Plan A," noted Steven Randall, an area manager. "Everyone has agreed that this plan is the best possible way to build a railcar."[17] Production stops if quality and safety are compromised. Dan Banks, son of Ralph Banks and vice president of operations of Trinity's Railcar Division, noted, "It wouldn't be effective if we didn't put some 'muscle' into it, which we do by giving every person the right to stop work on the product if it does not meet Plan A.... We've found over the last few years that production really is a byproduct of doing things right."[18]

The team concept was further extended with the introduction of Concurrent Product Development procedures. The concept was developed by Tim Wallace and Steve Smith in 1994. "The idea is to get all the parties that are involved in the project — engineering, manufacturing, purchasing and the customer — together. "The

whole design process involves everybody," noted Smith. "You have a faster design and a lower manufacturing cost, and the products are built with a minimal amount of problems."[19]

Trinity's self-improvement programs did not end at the factory floor. The company started an on-site day-care center in 1990, a step Ray Wallace deemed important to the company's future. "I think it's a great opportunity for us to help the young people that are there, but it also serves a very good purpose for the corporation as far as being able to offer our employees a place for them to leave their children in good care."[20]

Trinity also improved the way it purchased steel and other high-volume commodities by centralizing the functions for the corporation. "Everybody in the whole company was doing a little purchasing," Vice President Joe Piriano said. "Tim Wallace and Ray thought we should combine all of the divisions and have a central steel corporate purchasing. My main function is to negotiate all the contracts for the corporation on steel purchasing."[21]

Honoring Commitments

Both Ralph Banks and Ray Wallace were honored in 1992. Banks, a senior vice president, celebrated his 50th anniversary with the company on August 31, 1992. "I have enjoyed my years of working for Trinity, and if given the opportunity to

Above: Ralph Banks, left, and Ray Wallace were both honored in 1992. Banks was recognized for more than 50 years of service. Wallace was inducted into the Texas Business Hall of Fame.

Opposite: Poly Flo is the trademark name of a covered hopper car Trinity developed to transport plastic pellets and resins.

start my career again, I would make exactly the same choices," he noted.[22]

Ray Wallace, meanwhile, was among five members inducted into the Texas Business Hall of Fame. The others honored at a banquet in October 1992 were Houston oilman Roy Huffington; Ray Hunt of Dallas, chief executive of Hunt Oil Company; Drayton McLane, chief executive of Temple-based McLane Company, the nation's largest food distributor; and the Baird family of Fort Worth, whose Baird's Bakeries was the nation's largest family-owned bakery.[23]

A videotape made at the time of Wallace's induction included a brief history of Trinity and Wallace's business views. "We felt like any market that we were in, we needed to have a substantial portion of the market, try to be the leader in the market," he said.[24] Indeed, Trinity had become a leader in liquefied petroleum gas (LPG) containers, highway guardrail, marine vessels and railcar manufacturing through aggressive acquisitions and growth.

"We are basically a people business because what we build are generally mundane products, and they have to be built with quality, and they have to be built on the lowest-cost basis if you're going to stay in the marketplace. That's what made Trinity. That's what made the type and the quality of people that we have."[25]

With another transportation crisis pending, orders for grain hopper cars became especially vibrant. In March 1992, Burlington Northern, the nation's largest railroad company, selected Trinity to build 500 jumbo covered hopper cars for its grain-hauling fleet. The cars, worth more than $20 million, had 11 tons more capacity than the standard 100-ton-capacity jumbo hoppers. The Fort Worth–based Burlington Northern was the nation's largest grain carrier.[26] Within the following year, the railroad ordered 2,500 more cars. Nationwide, annual deliveries of railcars had nearly doubled to 48,819 vehicles.[27]

The Bessemer plant, however, did not join in this prosperous return of the market. On September 19, 1992, a bitter, at times violent, months-long strike began at the plant. About 500 members of the United Steelworkers of America struck over wages, health insurance and pension benefits. At one point in the confrontation, private security guards at the plant lobbed tear gas after strikers fired guns and slingshots and threw rocks and bottles.[28] As the strike dragged on, the company announced it would start to cut the workforce and close the plant by June 3, 1993. A newspaper reported that "reasons given are continuing financial losses and unforeseeable business circumstances related to the Steelworkers' strike."[29] The plant eventually reopened to produce parts for railcars.

Freight hauling of all kinds was growing as the national economy strengthened and as intermodal became accepted as the most efficient shipping method (see sidebar on page 118), and Trinity was benefiting. In 1994, TTX Company, known as Trailer Train until a name change in 1991, built up its intermodal fleet with orders for double-stack well cars, centerbeam lumber cars and all-purpose spine cars.[30]

THE FIFTH WAVE

INTERMODAL TRANSPORTATION IS ONE of the fastest growing areas for railroads. The U.S. Department of Transportation (DOT) considers this method a central part of "the fifth wave" of industrialization of the United States, putting intermodal transport in the august company of the Industrial Revolution, the second wave, and the growth of railroads, the third wave. (The first and fourth, respectively, are the location of great cities near seaports and trade routes and the massive investment in highway infrastructure.)[1]

But it wasn't until the 1980s that the intermodal concept was adopted on a widespread basis. The concept was actually introduced back in the 1920s, but fares were deemed too low by the Interstate Commerce Commission, and the practice was discouraged.

The idea refused to die. In 1953, the Southern Pacific Railroad pioneered the practice of "piggybacking" highway trailers on flatcars, a method that was soon adopted by most major railroads to compete with long-haul trucking on the new interstates.[2] Intermodal remained unpopular with railroad operators, however, because it required a higher level of quality service than they were accustomed to providing. Held in contempt, the "truck-train" department was in effect a railroader's purgatory, according to transportation writer Lawrence Kaufman, author of an editorial piece on the Intermodal Founding Fathers of North America Conference, held in August 1999.

"The founding fathers told fascinating stories of running afoul of senior executives and being exiled to the 'truck-train' departments, where it was expected that they would either leave the business or, at the very least, would never be heard from again. That strategy failed. With unconcealed pride, one speaker said: 'I want my tombstone to say, "He was a stubborn son-of-a-bitch."' "[3]

In 1984 intermodal transport came into its own with the growing movement toward containers. A company called American President Intermodal decided to use rail to ship goods that originated in Pacific Rim countries and were bound for the Midwestern and Eastern United States. Instead of using the Panama Canal to unload in ports close to the final destination, ships unloaded containers at ports along the West Coast. The containers then traveled by rail, double-stacked, to their destinations. It was a great success, and it wasn't long before rival companies adopted the practice.

A report published by the DOT in July 1999 emphasized how important it considered intermodal systems:

"As the 20th century ends, the United States is in a fifth wave of industrialization that is transforming the global market and changing traditional notions of development. This wave is based on innovations in logistics and manufacturing.... Now, more than ever, businesses require a seamless, intermodal transportation system."[4]

Cornering the Market

Ray Wallace pursued the same strategy in the marine segment as he had with railcars. When barge output had dwindled to just 45 vessels in 1987, Wallace saw, in his words, a "once-in-a-lifetime opportunity" when his competitors saw only red ink. Shipyards all along the Gulf Coast sat idle, their machinery rusting and their workers, a tremendous pool of talent, seeking their livelihoods elsewhere.

Trinity bought up shipyards and marine-related area companies as fast as possible, then turned those assets into leaner, more efficient organizations, which prompted one New Orleans newspaper writer to describe Trinity Marine, the subsidiary under which all marine activities were organized, as "a rare phenomenon — a profitable shipbuilder. Based in Gulfport, Mississippi, Trinity Marine has built success by combining centralized management with small shipyards not dependent for markets on any single industry, customer or variety of vessel."[31]

Many shipyards worked just to break even, and at least a quarter were idle. About half of Trinity Marine's boat yards were devoted to building and repairing barges. Trinity Marine mainly built barges and supply boats, but its products included other types. It had recently completed a 322-foot-long gambling boat that carried gaming machines and 3,500 passengers. The boat, delivered in New Orleans, cost $50 million. The company also had a $20 million order from the U.S. Navy for four 82-foot high-speed patrol boats.[32]

By 1995, Ray Wallace had managed to corner the barge market for as little as $100 million. With 18 shipyards, half of the Gulf Coast's entire boat-building capacity, Trinity awaited the return of the market, just as it had with railcars.[33] "If you're in a replacement business, you just have to let time work for you," Wallace noted. "We've always lined up with the contrarians."[34]

Cementing Relationships

Trinity strengthened its capacity in structural products through a merger with Ohio-based Syro Steel Company, a leader in bridge rail and guardrails. Trinity acquired all of Syro's common stock in exchange for 1.6 million shares of Trinity stock, which was worth about $50 million.[35] Syro, which had sales of $82 million in 1991, became a subsidiary of Trinity. The firm, founded in 1937, worked with Southwest Research Institute in San Antonio and Texas A&M University's Texas Transportation Institute, and the relationships continued after the merger.

Syro Steel Company, acquired by Trinity in 1995, was a pioneer in the development of guardrails and had longstanding relationships with state and federal highway safety agencies.

RAY BURTON AND TTX

THE WORD "INTERMODAL" may have been dirty among railroaders, but that didn't stop a few visionaries from pursuing ways to make it profitable. One of the most successful is Raymond C. Burton.

Burton is a pioneer in the railroad industry. He knows well the sting of the arrows that are so often flung at the backs of pioneers. In the late 1960s, Burton saw a way to marry the capabilities of a newfangled gadget called the computer to the needs of Sante Fe Railroad, where he worked after receiving his MBA from Wharton School of Business in 1963.

Burton overcame resistance to develop the first computer program for the distribution of intermodal equipment. "Many railroad people at that time didn't look at [intermodal] as real railroading," Burton said. "It was a little like 'real men don't eat quiche Lorraine.' "[1]

Nonetheless, the marriage of intermodal and computer technology was a success, improving Sante Fe's container utilization by 18 percent. After an eight-year stint as an executive with Burlington Northern Railroad, Burton joined TTX, then known as Trailer Train. He faced his biggest challenge.

Trailer Train had been founded in 1956 by a consortium of 39 railroads (with the blessing of the federal government) in response to shippers' slowly growing interest in intermodal transportation. The company was vital to the health of the entire railroad industry. When Burton took control as president in 1982, that health was seriously threatened. Burdened by the

Trailer Train

Harry Syak, Syro president and grandson of a founding member, said the two firms were compatible. "Combining our forces will add a new dimension to Trinity," Syak said.[36] Syro had been a pioneer in the research and development of safer guardrails and highway cushions to reduce injuries and save lives.

Trinity entered an entirely new area in 1991 when it purchased Transit Mix Concrete Company. Transit Mix Concrete was founded 52 years ago in Beaumont, Texas. Ray Wallace appointed state Rep. Mark Stiles, a Democratic lawmaker, president of the concrete company. Stiles had been its vice president and general manager and had helped

negotiate the sale. Warren Goehringer, president of Transit Mix, remained as a consultant. Although it was a new venture, Dean Phelps, a Trinity vice president, said the concrete operation fit well into the company's structural products segment. The company also was optimistic about the growth potential in South Texas, where it had its Beaumont shipyard, as well as its railcar repair plant in Vidor, just east of Beaumont.[37]

The actual sale of the company was somewhat unusual because Ray Wallace had decided he wanted Stiles, one of the partners in Transit Mix, to run the concrete business. After an all-night negotiating session, Wallace told the nego-

debt of its two subsidiaries, Railgon and Railbox, Trailer Train was on the brink of disaster.

Burton managed to restructure the debt and turn the company around, for which he earned *Railway Age* magazine's 1986 "Railroader of the Year" Award. (He won it again in 1992, one of only three people to win twice.) But even as he was lauded for turning Trailer Train

into a success, Burton recognized that the fundamental way goods were being transported across the country would have to change because the United States had become a substantial importer. Once again, he weathered the arrows of naysayers by investing early in double-stack well cars (see sidebar on page 118).

"We had made a study in the mid-eighties that showed the double-stack was becoming more popular," he noted in a 1999 interview. "I said that if we don't grasp this concept and embrace it fully, we're not going to have much of a future."[2]

Trailer Train, which changed its name to TTX in 1991, also embraced other designs, such as the all-purpose spine car. The spine car was developed with the help of Trinity. Working together, the companies developed the design within six months and soon rendered the single-stack well car and flat cars obsolete.

"They're honest people," Burton said. "They live up to their word, and they're good people to do business with. I respect Ray and Tim from a business standpoint, and I consider them friends."[3]

A spine car, used to transport truck trailers by rail. The car was built for Trailer Train, now known as TTX.

tiators that Stiles would conclude the agreement. "He had a lot of faith in me, but he knew I was going to be with this for the long run," said Stiles in 1999. "I was able to negotiate with my partners to buy the company for Trinity."[38]

Some were surprised and advised Ray Wallace against getting into a non-steel business. But Stiles said Ray Wallace was an unparalleled teacher with special business-building talents. "We have taken the values that he put in Trinity, the manufacturing standards, and put them into what was always looked at as a mom-and-pop individual industry like the concrete and aggregate business," he said.[39] Stiles later asked Wallace about expansion plans.

"He said to me, 'Do you think that I let you buy that company for Trinity for it to stay the same size?' So we started on a journey that has led to where we weren't in the sand business five years ago, and we're the largest concrete sand manufacturer in the state of Texas now, and we're probably the 14th or 15th largest sand and gravel producer in the United States [as of 1999]."[40]

Over the coming years, Transit Mix, as a Trinity subsidiary, bought up other concrete and materials operations in other parts of Texas. Transit Mix bought the Central Texas Division of Tarmac Texas, Inc., in September 1992. A couple

of months later, in November 1992, it bought Cowboy Concrete Corporation, one of its major local competitors.[41]

Transit Mix expanded its Central Texas presence with the purchase in early 1993 of Waco Ready Mix Company and its associated mining operations for sand and gravel. The subsidiary moved further westward in Texas, acquiring assets of South Texas Construction Company as well as various assets of Bernath Concrete Products and Brazos Valley Lumber.

In the fall of 1993, Transit Mix bought B&M Sand and Gravel, Inc., and assets of American Ready-Mix, a division of Bluebonnet Paving. B&M, headquartered in Rockwall, Texas, provided sand, gravel, and special mixes of sand and soil products. These products were used in golf courses, masonry sand and loam for lawn care. In 1994, Transit Mix expanded its operations beyond Texas to Louisiana.

In late 1994, Transit Mix announced it had bought certain assets of Lafarge Corporation, part of the Lafarge Coppee group in Paris, France. Nearly all of the operations bought from Lafarge in the $30 million deal were in Texas.

It was not unusual that Trinity was buying foreign-owned cement plants in its own home state. Most of the American cement industry was in foreign hands, including holdings by the French giant, Lafarge. Overseas companies had invested in cement businesses in the United States when cement was in oversupply and prices low. But cement prices in the United States were rising with the recovering economy. The world also was going through one of the biggest building booms in history as developing countries built highways, dams, airports, power plants and other structures. As a 1994 article noted, "global cement consumption is some 1.4 billion tons ... and has been growing at an annual rate of 3.6 percent a year, faster than the consumption of other basic commodities like steel and copper."[42]

The Lafarge transaction involved 24 ready-mix concrete operations in Texas, four aggregate oper-

Trinity's entry into the cement business surprised many and alarmed some because it was a non-steel enterprise. But the business fit well with the company's construction segment.

ations in Texas and an aggregate operation in Indian Village, Louisiana. The move expanded and strengthened Transit Mix's presence in Central and Eastern Texas, as well as in Louisiana. With the acquisition, one analyst noted, "Trinity has more cement trucks in Texas than Texas Industries," which described itself as the largest producer of cement in Texas.[43] One of the ready-mix plants was in Longview, where Trinity's five other plants built tank car parts and the cars themselves.

Mexico

Up until 1995, Trinity Industries operated only in the United States. Ray Wallace and Trinity had been investors in steel fabricating operations in Mexico since the fifties. But on May 5, Trinity became an international company when it purchased all of the capital stock of the holding company that owned Grupo TATSA S.A. de C.V. in exchange for 1.2 million shares of Trinity stock. Grupo TATSA, headquartered in Mexico City, manufactured and distributed fabricated steel products, including LPG containers, rail tank car barrels and heads.

Manuel Castro, who had been the head of Grupo TATSA since 1958, said in an interview that Ray Wallace had been concerned that Trinity's competitors might purchase railcar components from Grupo TATSA.

Castro and Wallace were already partners in an LP tank venture in Mexico called Cabezas de Acero Kikipoo. By agreement, the Mexican company stayed out of the United States. Castro owned a 51 percent interest in Cabezas de Acero Kikipoo. Wallace owned 49 percent in the venture.

TATSA had plants in Mexico City and Huehuetoca, a small town just outside Mexico City. TATSA's products were used in Mexico, the United States and other Latin American markets, including Brazil, Chile, Peru and Costa Rica. The tank barrels and LPG tanks made in the Mexican plants were shipped to Trinity plants in Longview and Beaumont for completion. With the acquisition, Grupo TATSA became Trinity Industries de Mexico. TATSA had revenues of about $50 million annually, and the transaction was valued at between $40 million and $50 million.[44]

The expansion into Mexico was just the beginning of Trinity's growth in the international arena. All over the world, political and economic barriers were falling and new opportunities were growing. With the old guard retiring in the twilight of the first millennium, Trinity would navigate these unfamiliar waters under a new generation of leadership.

Liquefied petroleum gas tanks undergo inspection at Grupo TATSA in Mexico City. Trinity acquired TATSA in 1995.

In 1997, Grupo TATSA began manufacturing hopper cars. In the latter part of the nineties, Trinity expanded its global presence.

CHAPTER TWELVE

A GLOBAL PRESENCE

"We will forever be in awe of the mastery that Ray Wallace demonstrated in inspiring every employee of this company to achieve excellence...."

— Tribute to Ray Wallace, 1999[1]

THE AVERAGE LENGTH OF time a chief executive officer handles the helm of a major American corporation is about eight years. In July 1998, W. Ray Wallace announced that after 40 years as CEO of Trinity, he believed it was time for him to pass the reins, effective at the end of that year.

Tim Wallace, who had been appointed president and chief operating officer of Trinity two years earlier, succeeded him in a transfer of power and responsibilities that took place seamlessly and in good order. Speaking for the board, Jess Hay, a director since the original 1958 merger of Trinity and Dallas Tank, said the smooth transition was an enduring tribute to Ray Wallace.

"The board shares Ray's enthusiasm for Tim Wallace's capabilities and for the entire group of Trinity's outstanding operating managers. Tim has evidenced finely tuned business skills throughout his 23-year career at Trinity, and he has been a forceful and creative leader since becoming president and chief operating officer in 1996. Thus, when Ray retires in December, he will leave the company in good and dependable hands."[2]

Hay's comments were made at the annual meeting of shareholders in 1998. Interviewed several months later that year, Hay gave a less formal appraisal of Ray Wallace's decision to step down.

"You can get to a point where you think you're indispensable. Ray never thought that way. I think he stayed until he felt like things were in good hands and until his successor management team was ready to take over."[3]

In a 1999 interview, Ray Wallace said, "I personally feel that if you have management that's ready for a task and hold them too long in a treading-water position, they're going to either lose their enthusiasm or go elsewhere."[4]

When he retired, the elder Wallace left a company that was closing in on $3 billion in revenue and was the leader in the markets it served. Tim Wallace took over a company that was just beginning to grow internationally, a trend he accelerated as Trinity was entering the new millennium.

Thinking Globally

Trinity had been involved with Mexico one way or the other since its beginning, but the company essentially remained a North American entity until 1996. That year, Trinity acquired Transcisco Industries in a $47 million stock swap, a transac-

Liquefied petroleum gas is a growing business in Latin America, where natural gas lines are scarce. Besides its ease of transportation, LPG is also friendly to the environment.

tion that gave Trinity a sizable interest in Russia's largest railcar manufacturer, SFAT. In a country that is roughly 6,000 miles wide and where highways are scarce, rail is Russia's transportation lifeblood. Russia has more than 2.2 million miles of rail. The United States, by comparison, has about half that. Bill Neewby, vice president in charge of international sales and marketing, said SFAT was a bright spot in the uncertain terrain of the former Soviet Union. "Even through the bad times, we're continuing to grow its asset base. It's been a very good investment for us."[5]

Neewby said he expects the current crises in Russia and the other members of the Commonwealth of Independent States to eventually ease, and when they do, the growth opportunities will be tremendous.

"Russia is the richest country in the world today in raw materials. Since 1917, their policy has been not to export their raw materials but to only use what they needed. So any commodity you can think of, it has. The culture won't change to a free market system overnight, but the younger generation has tasted freedom and they'll work through their present problems."[6]

Building a capitalist base upon the ruins of communism took some interesting turns in Eastern Europe. One of these was Trinity's majority stock purchase of the Romanian railcar company called Astra Vagoane, the leading railcar maker in Europe. Under the old communist system, Romania had been designated as one of the major railcar manufacturing centers, so resources and training had been directed to that end. Astra Vagoane was one of three large and well-equipped railcar plants in that country and was ideally located in the city of Arad, which can ship cars efficiently to the growing markets in Western Europe. "Its location is just one of Arad's advantages," noted Doug Schneider, vice president in charge of the Romanian plant. "It's also an area whose people have a good work ethic, heavy technical training and low costs. All of this is coming at a time when we feel the market for railcars is starting to open very quickly in the West."[7]

In September 1999, Tim Wallace announced Trinity's intention to purchase a second Romanian railcar plant, MEVA, S.A. This plant was located along the Danube River in the town of Drobeta Turnu Severin. With a backlog of 2,000 orders for railcars, Wallace noted that the second purchase would solidify Romania as Trinity's base for railcar production and repair.

The plants and equipment in both were old, however, and Trinity committed about $10 million to refurbish the plant and adopt quality and management programs used with great success elsewhere. "We absolutely have committed to making them world-class manufacturing facilities," said Schneider. "What we've done is taken the template of our manufacturing facility here and just picked it up and moved it over there."[8]

This was the plan Trinity pursued in 1997 when the company set up railcar production lines in Mexico. Managers replicated all the processes, quality control programs, job standards and safety programs in Longview, Texas, and transferred them to Mexico. The learning curve was sharp, and in early 1998, the first of the 5161-type grain cars rolled off the lines at Trinity Industries de Mexico to fulfill an order from GATX.[9] Orders quickly flowed in from both the United States and Latin America. A joint venture between Kansas City Southern Industries and Transportacion Maritima Mexico resulted in the first cars to be built and put into service entirely in Mexico.[10]

The processes extended to the international tank business as well. The high price of gasoline and the stringent pollution regulations in Mexico led to a jump in the production of LPG tanks, from 1,500 to more than 5,000 per month.[11] Also, the Mexican government began a program to replace residential propane cylinders, used for cooking, if they were more than 12 years old. Trinity Industries de Mexico was the largest LPG tank manufacturer in that country.[12]

Trinity moved into Latin American markets with the purchase of an LPG manufacturing plant in Brazil, whose people are beyond the reach of natural gas lines. Like many people in the developing areas of South America, Brazilians depend on LPG for cooking and heating. Trinity later added a second plant in Brazil to build tank containers for home use. In December 1998, the company announced that its subsidiary, Trinity Rail do Brasil, had entered into a joint venture agreement with Companhia Comercio e Construcoes of Brazil, or CCC, to build railcars there. The partnership was formed to build 300 grain cars for Ferronorte S.A., the country's newest railroad. (CCC, based in Rio de Janeiro, was one of Brazil's largest railcar builders with three manufacturing plants. It had been building railcars for more than 40 years.)

Rails to Riches

In the United States, orders for new railcars were beginning to arrive faster than Trinity could fill them. One magazine article noted the "ironic twist of fate for American railroads. After decades of decline, railroads are back. Today, they transport 84 percent more freight (measured in ton-miles) than they did ... at the height of World War II."[13] A nationwide shortage of cars in 1997 was blamed on underestimated demand for new intermodal railcars and the need to modernize and standardize fleets following several major railroad mergers. Burlington Northern, for instance, had merged with Santa Fe Railroad Company, which required the new railroad to replace its older and smaller-capacity units in the combined 33,000-grain-car fleet. As a result, Trinity received an initial order for 6,000 covered grain hopper cars in October 1997. One month later, TTX, which had purchased almost 1,500 spine cars that year, ordered another 2,000 intermodal spine cars. Fina Oil Company ordered 1,200 railcars from Trinity, which included the new plastic pellet cars, a design that increased capacity by 10 percent.[14]

The year 1998 saw a continuation of the railcar boom, with orders for 15,000 more cars of vary-

ing types arriving in the first three months alone. Trinity hired more workers to tackle its biggest backlog in years. An analyst attributed the increased orders for railcar manufacturers like Trinity to "the aging of the nation's railcar fleet, a hot economy pushing demand for rail cargo capacity, and fierce competition among transporters and shippers to improve service."[15]

On October 15, 1998, Trinity presented the 25,000th tank car to GATX since the two began their unique relationship in 1984. "Together, we have reached an impressive milestone which is an example of two companies continuously improving

Above: When Trinity delivered GATX's 25,000th car, a green and blue commemorative railcar was built to mark the occasion. The actual 25,000th car is black.

Below: The latest plastic pellet–car design increased carrying capacity by 10 percent.

their relationship over time," Tim Wallace said.[16] Ward Fuller, president and CEO of General American, described the longtime teamwork as a "tremendous success."[17] A ceremony to mark the event was held at Trinity's Longview plant with lunch for 600 guests, plant representatives and corporate representatives. Trinity displayed a green and blue commemorative car, as well as the actual 25,000th car, which would be used by Minnesota Corn Processors. Fuller gave a $25,000 check to the Boys and Girls Clubs of Gregg County in honor of the delivery of the 25,000th car.[18]

More than two-thirds of the cars that Trinity manufactured for GATX up to that point had been built in the last six years. Between 1984 and 1991, the years of lean orders, GATX bought a total of 8,000 cars from Trinity. From 1992 to 1998, as orders for replacement and technologically advanced cars increased industry-wide, GATX purchased 17,000 more.[19]

Fuller also attributed the increased orders to GATX's working relationship with Trinity, which included similar attitudes about the workers who built the railcars. "In our organization," Fuller explained, "I'm on the bottom of our organization chart, and our customers are on the top, and all of our true artists and experts are in between, and

probably that stems from my blue-collar background and working in a steel mill during school as a boilermaker.... I've always had tremendous respect for everyone I've worked with."[20]

He found a kindred spirit in Tim Wallace, he noted.

"It was very interesting in my first time at Longview to see how Tim really respected his workers. He got a lot of grease on his hands that day, talked to a lot of people. He didn't usher me through the facility but let me wander in and talk to people on my own, and that meant a lot to me. It was very apparent that Tim and I both shared a common understanding, and that was a respect for the real artists and experts that we work with. That gave me a lot of confidence in terms of having a long-term relationship and expanding our relationship with Trinity."[21]

The Aluminum Revolution

Of all the varied cargo carried by rail, coal still accounted for more than 40 percent of the tonnage shipped by railcars. Railcars once flowed from Appalachia to bring coal to utilities, but the passage of increasingly more stringent Clean Air acts in the 1990s prompted customers to turn to

Below: An aging fleet, underestimated demand and a hot economy spurred orders for railcars of all types, such as the GATX Tank Train shown below.

THE RIGHT COMBINATION

THE 6,000 CARS BURLINGTON NORTHern Sante Fe ordered from Trinity was the single largest order BNSF has ever placed with one supplier. But these types of large orders for specific types of cars will become more common as the railroad industry consolidates.

"As the industry has consolidated, our supplier base has also consolidated," explained Matt Rose, BNSF's president and COO.

"It forces people to understand the needs of their partners in the industry for a longer term than the year-to-year transactional needs. Certain suppliers have competencies in certain product likes and, of course, our goal is to make sure we team up with those suppliers."[1]

In Trinity's case, the 6,000-car order was filled over a three-year period. Beginning in 1998,

Trinity delivered 2,000 cars each year. What drew BNSF to Trinity was its capacity, customer focus and engineering ability. "They have the capacity to handle this kind of order," said Rose. "And they are always looking at innovative issues for us."[2]

The type of covered hopper car BNSF was seeking was one built of lighter but stronger material that would allow the company to transport more grain. The result was a car capable of carrying 5,160 cubic feet of grain, as opposed to 4,750 cubic feet of grain. Weighing 286,000 pounds fully loaded, the car could safely travel on BNSF's tracks.

"They just hit on the right combination in literally all areas on this car," Rose noted. "So instead of apportioning the order out in the conventional way, we sort of stepped up to the plate and allowed it to be single sourced. It was the right thing to do."[3]

---

low-sulfur coal, which was found in great quantity in Wyoming and other Western states. The snag was finding a way to transport enough low-sulfur coal to make it economical while staying within federal safety limits regulating gross weight for railcars.

The solution was an aluminum hopper body on steel components. This innovation permitted Trinity to increase payload by 20 percent. "Old all-steel cars weighed 55,000 pounds," explained Trinity engineer Steve Smith. "These weigh maybe 43,000 pounds. You get to deliver an extra 12,000 pounds per trip. That represents a huge amount of money."[22]

The aluminum solution also benefited another market segment, plastic pellet cars. Plastic pellets were normally carried by all-steel cars lined with a coating to protect the product from impurities. Using aluminum, however, allowed a shipper to move greater quantities of pellets meant for the medical industry. Car linings have a limited life, and when they break down, many of the pellets

can become contaminated. An all-aluminum car was inherently cleaner than a steel one and would not react chemically with the plastic.

Trinity's latest generation of Rapid Discharge cars, the RD5, were made of aluminum and could carry up to 4,600 cubic feet. At a maximum weight of 47,000 pounds, these cars were a major improvement over the previous 65,000-pound all-steel Rapid Discharge units. The car could hold more coal because "we creatively changed the thickness of the side posts on the outside of the car to where we kept the extreme width of the car the same. But the inside of the box is much wider, and we did that by making wider, thinner side posts on the outside of the car," noted Wayne Hacker, vice president of Trinity's coal business unit.[23]

At the old Mosher Steel plant on Maple Avenue in Dallas, in early 1999, workers were building a new articulated, double-stacked container well car that consisted of three 53-foot unit cars. In the past, Trinity had built well cars, primarily five-unit,

Lighter and stronger than steel, aluminum cars allowed Trinity to increase payload by 20 percent. This made the transport of relatively clean-burning coal from the West more economically feasible.

48-foot cars. However, it had built only a few well cars since 1991, instead concentrating on spine cars. But the use of double-stack container shipping instead of trailers and single-level containers was rising. "Spine cars have probably run their route as far as demand is concerned for the next five years because trailer loading in the industry has pretty much leveled off," said Don Bodinger, general manager of Trinity's intermodal strategic business unit. "But container hauling is forecasted to continue to rise through the next decade."[24]

The Maple Avenue plant had to be retooled for the new cars. "We shipped our last spine car, which is a model that we built prior to the well car,... at the end of April [1999]," said plant manager Todd

Lokash. "As soon as we were finished in the stations with the last parts for the last car, we started tearing them out. So it was pretty well-timed and planned out.... It's a big project, and you're going to run into snags and changes but ... everybody from corporate, everybody from the plants, all the support groups from corporate, everybody just stuck together, got their hands dirty and got it done."[25] Some prototypes of the newly designed well cars were shipped to TTX in early September 1999.

Spinning Off Halter Marine

In 1996, Trinity began spinning off Halter Marine along with Trinity Marine's oceangoing marine businesses. "Halter was more valuable under public ownership than as an integral part of Trinity," wrote Ray Wallace in his letter to shareholders.[26] The stock sale, completed in early 1997, generated about $35 million, which more than covered debts to Trinity Industries.

Wallace had found both the power boat and the structural steel businesses lacking the repetitive characteristics that had fueled Trinity's growth. "The powerboat business was something that I never felt Trinity developed a lot of expertise in other than the people that we had acquired," he said in a 1999 interview. "We didn't ever seem to add to those entities to the degree that we historically had been able to add to other

A tank barge under construction at Trinity's plant in Ashland City, Tennessee.

GUARDRAILS

IN THE FIFTIES, LUMBERING CHEVROLETS ruled the road. In the sixties, the name of the game was high performance, with Ford Mustangs and Chevy Camaros battling for the hearts of motorists. Then OPEC turned off the oil taps in the seventies, and suddenly small, zippy economy cars dashed along highways. By the 1990s, the sport-utility vehicle was the new rage.

Each decade has brought a new design to meet the needs and the desires of the public. As the look and size of automobiles changed, so did the safety requirements for guardrails. "We had a road system that was designed for Elvis' Cadillac," explained Don Graham, group vice president of the guardrail group. "When Elvis' Cadillac hit that guardrail, it slowed him down. It redirected him. It kept him from going through the guardrail.... When the little car hit the guardrail, it got right in the car with the driver because the little car didn't have enough force to crush the guardrail."[1]

A study by the Insurance Institute for Highway Safety found that more than one in four deaths on U.S. roads occurred because of collisions with roadside objects like guardrails. The report gave a chilling summary: "Years ago when vehicles crashed into the end of an older guardrail, the rail would act as a spear going through the vehicle. As an alternative, a rail with ends that slope down into the ground was developed to cure the spearing problem, but unfortunately a new problem arose — vaulting and rolling. When vehicles collide with the turned-down end, they sometimes fly into the air and roll, sometimes causing the passenger to be ejected from the vehicle."[2]

The Texas Transportation Institute, or TTI, established in 1950, had joined with the Texas Department of Transportation to develop a guardrail end treatment that would make accidents survivable. One such development was the ET2000 guardrail end treatment. When a car hit the ET2000, its energy became "absorbed as the rail is pushed through an extruder, which flattens the rail, bends it and forces it away from the vehicle. As the railing curls away from the vehicle toward the roadside, energy is absorbed, bringing the vehicle to a safe stop."[3] TTI teamed with Syro Steel to produce ET2000s on an experimental basis. The first samples were installed in Texas in June 1990.

In 1998, the Federal Highway Administration launched a major initiative to improve highway guardrail standards. Trinity continued Syro Steel's cooperative efforts to improve safety by providing state and federal agencies with manufacturing ability. Charlie Wooten, director emeritus of the Texas Transportation Institute, noted that "Trinity has done an excellent job of seeing that these products are getting put into use. That's something we could never do by ourselves."[4]

acquisitions, and that was one of the motivating forces of separation of the power boat and the barge business."[27]

Halter Marine took 10 of the Trinity Marine shipyards in the spinoff, including the Gretna yard at Harvey, Louisiana, and Equitable's Industrial Canal shipyard, the site of the old Higgins yard. Trinity mainly kept the barge yards. Trinity and Halter Marine continued to work together. At the time of the spinoff, Halter had a contract to build 180 inland barges on order at Trinity.

Following the sale, Trinity reorganized its businesses into three segments: transportation products (railcars, marine products and leasing operations), construction products (ready-mix concrete and aggregate, plus highway safety products and custom-rolled structural shapes) and industrial products (metal components group and Trinity's traditional gas container products).

Throughout 1997, Trinity or its subsidiaries bought companies in each of its business segments. Key acquisitions included the Industrial Products Division of the Wisconsin-based Ladish Company, a leading manufacturer of pipefittings, flanges and valves. With the purchase, Trinity possessed the broadest offering of fittings and flanges of any producer in North America.[28] Transit Mix, meanwhile, bought some of the assets of Industrial Companies Inc. The purchase included five ready-mix plants and a sand and gravel operation in and around Baton Rouge.

Other acquisitions included Differential Holdings, Inc., parent of Difco, Inc., a specialty railcar manufacturer located in Findlay, Ohio, and assets of Busch Mechanical Services, a railcar rebuilding plant in Springfield, Missouri.

The Foundry Business

In fall 1998, Trinity took its first dive into the foundry business when it bought MCT Holdings, Inc., the parent of McConway & Torley, which was the largest manufacturer of railcar couplers in the United States. In 1999, Trinity bought a second foundry, this one in Anniston, Alabama, and made railcar parts there.

A Trinity news release said that the Pittsburgh-based McConway & Torley was "recognized as the premier domestic manufacturer of railcar

The acquisition of Industrial Products meant that Trinity held the widest product line of valves, fittings and flanges in the nation.

coupler systems."[29] The firm, with 625 employees and annual revenues of about $80 million, had major casting plants in Kutztown and Pittsburgh. McConway & Torley became a Trinity subsidiary with Buddy Bell remaining as its president.

The invention of automatic couplers, which joined railcars, was among the major improvements to railcar safety. Before Confederate veteran Eli H. Janney invented the first effective automatic coupler, which resembled the hooked fingers of two hands, the link-and-pin method, along with the hand brake, had "kept all rail service slow and hazardous," according to John F. Stover, author of *American Railroads*. "The link-and-pin coupler was so arranged that the brakeman had to stand between the cars in order to steer the link into the socket and drop the pin. This job was so dangerous that brakemen were often recognized by missing fingers or a crippled hand."[30]

Janney, an ex-farmer and dry-goods clerk, whittled his first coupler model with a penknife, patented his device in 1868 and improved it by 1873. In 1877, "He fell under the protective wing of William McConway and John J. Torley, " wrote John H. White, Jr., in his book on 19th century American freight cars.[31] White also said that McConway and Torley were "practical mechanics; they understood tooling, material strength, and just where to add metal or take it away. They could thus guide Janney in the bench-work improvements so necessary to make his coupler a workaday success."[32] A standard coupler, based on Janney's model, went into widespread use with the passage of 1893 federal legislation requiring the use of automatic couplers, as well as air brakes, on all trains.

McConway & Torley began operations just a few years after the Civil War as a hardware manufacturer. In 1869, William McConway joined the newly organized Pittsburgh firm of Lewis and Company, which included John J. Torley and Samuel Lewis. By the time the company incorporated in 1887, Lewis had withdrawn from the business and Torley had died. The company's primary business initially was harness fittings but it later made railway supplies, including couplers. A 1945 book titled *Men and Women of Wartime Pittsburgh and Environs* noted that "the corporation has shipped couplers all over the world, including Australia, Africa, Russia,

China and India. Over ninety percent of the railroad cars in China before the outbreak of the war there were equipped with McConway & Torley couplers."[33]

The book described McConway & Torley as an "internationally known manufacturer of carbon and alloy steel castings.... The normal peacetime production of the corporation consists mainly of railway steel castings; that is, automatic couplers, coupler yokes, side frames and bolsters, and miscellaneous car and locomotive castings."[34] During World War II, the company made armor castings for Army tanks; castings for boats, guns and gun mounts; and castings for locomotives used by the United States armed forces, as well as those of Russia, France and others. "It supplied virtually all the armor castings used on the M-5 tanks built by the Cadillac division of the General Motors Corporation. These were the tanks that chased the German general, Rommel, out of Africa."[35]

A Transit Mix crew pours concrete for the foundation of a new school.

Prepared for the Future

In 1999, Trinity Industries was nearing the $3 billion mark, with revenues rising 19 percent over the previous year to $2.93 billion. Tim Wallace continued to develop the new generation of Trinity leadership and to hone the executive suite by recruiting proven talent to join him in his mission of providing results, improving and growing the company.

During the mid 1990s, as Tim began to assume broader operational responsibilities, he realized the importance of locating additional executives who could grow with his plans for diversified expansion. His plan also provided the opportunity to free key individuals to allow them to use their experience in other areas of the company.

In the mid-1990s, John Nussrallah joined Trinity from Conrail. His first assignment was as manager of a railcar manufacturing facility. Nussrallah was eventually promoted to president of the Railcar Group. Today, as a key member of Wallace's executive operations team, Nussrallah supports Trinity's plan to diversify its earnings base. As Trinity enters the 21st century, its leadership plans to continue the shift of its product mix as it has demonstrated its ability to do so many times before.

Nussrallah explained that his organization is focused on becoming a full-service vendor for the railroads, which includes a variety of services. "We are listening to our customers and targeting specific services, which will help them become more efficient," said Nussrallah.[36]

Nussrallah put together a strong management team. His business unit presidents are Jeff Marsh, Pat Wallace and George Creighton. Marsh, a former Campbell Taggert executive, joined Trinity in the mid-1990s. He initially took responsibility for Trinity's railcar purchasing function. Over time, he assumed operating responsibilities for the tank car and pellet business units.

Cross-functional teams have enabled Trinity to improve productivity and quality, and enabled workers to be flexible enough to jump to different designs, like this combo car.

LD LMT
LT WT
EXW.   10-08
EW.   10-00
CU. FT. 6100
734400
194700
91300

Pat Wallace, Tim's older brother, is playing a role in helping to shape Trinity's future. Pat had departed from the company in the late 1980s until the mid-1990s to pursue other interests. Tim Wallace asked him to return to create and lead Trinity's organizational development function. Pat Wallace now heads the freight car business unit.

John Nussrallah knew where to go when it was time to bring in someone to run Trinity's rail services and parts business unit. He reached for former Conrail colleague George Creighton. Growth in rail services is a key part of Trinity's strategic plan, and Creighton is positioned to develop this business segment.

Still focused on his long-term plan with the notion of expanding globally, Wallace encouraged Doug Schneider to join the company. In the early 1990s, when Wallace met Schneider, he was impressed with Schneider's leadership and management skills. Schneider initially joined the company as head of one of Trinity's larger railcar plants. This was the first time Schneider had ever seen a railcar from a manufacturing point of view.

Schneider began with the Railcar Group and later moved into barges. He improved safety, labor efficiency, inventory control and on-time shipments. He did it by instituting measures that are still reviewed on a regular basis, a continuous program of self-improvement. "I believe anything you measure gets better," he said. Schneider, who is now president of Trinity's Inland Barge Group and international ventures, had previously worked for a British conglomerate called BTR as a group president in charge of five different divisions.[37]

As he assembled the members of his team, Wallace developed an overall strategy to encourage them to take chances. This is the foundation of Wallace's entrepreneurial vision, explained Senior Vice President Mark Stiles.

"Anyone can sit back in a position with no pressure and be told what to do every day. Tim wants people to take those risks and identify where we are today, show where we want to be tomorrow, and then explain how we're going to get there. The world is at our fingertips."[38]

Stiles joined Trinity in 1991 when Ray Wallace acquired the Beaumont, Texas-based Transit Mix Concrete Company. Stiles was a prominent Texas legislator for more than 17 years, representing the Beaumont area district. In 1999, Wallace asked Stiles to relocate to the corporate office. Stiles has become an important part of Wallace's new generation of leaders. He has continued to assume a broader role within the company. In addition, Stiles took on the challenge of heading Trinity's Shared Services Operations.

Another member of the team, Manuel Castro, had been associated with Trinity since the late 1950s when he led Grupo TATSA, of which Ray Wallace was a partner. Castro was a young engineer to whom Ray Wallace had assumed the role of mentor. Trinity later acquired full interest in Grupo TATSA, which is now called Trinity Industries de Mexico, and Castro eventually became president of Worldwide LPG.

Castro's technical background, along with his years of experience and learning under Wallace, has positioned him well to hand off to two other young talents now understudying Castro. Jess Collins joined Trinity in the early 1990s after several years in the aerospace industry. He has assumed roles in several of Trinity's businesses including railcar and marine, and even an international assignment. He is now business unit president of U.S. LPG.

In the mid-1990s, Castro recruited Antonio Carillo, an industrial engineer from Mexico City who received an MBA in finance and operations from Wharton and later earned his CPA designation. Carillo is executive vice president and general manager of Mexico where he brings his conceptual thought processes to manufacturing methods.

Jim Ivy joined Trinity as chief financial officer in 1998. Though officially a newcomer to Trinity, he was in fact familiar with the company. While at Ernst and Young, Ivy was on the Trinity account for more than 30 years and worked closely with Ken Lewis, a longtime Trinity executive who succeeded Ed Breeding. (Breeding retired in 1986 as CFO after 24 years of service to Trinity. Lewis retired in 1996 after more than 20 years of service.)

As an outsider, Ivy assumed that Trinity, with its astounding success, had its share of the cumbersome bureaucracy that often comes with growth. His perception changed quickly upon joining the organization.

"You just think something has more bureau-cratic structure and processes because of their size. At first, I didn't see how completely Trinity was an entrepreneurial type of company with almost every-thing that implies — entrepreneurial and at the same time, informal. You don't have a bunch of people papering every decision that was made. It's made and you go on to get the benefits of it. It's a very results-focused organization."[39]

Recognizing the need for balance in both cor-porate freedom and corporate structure, Wallace brought in Mike Fortado as general counsel and corporate secretary to lead this new function. Previously, this role was handled by outside counsel. Fortado had been a senior executive with a Dallas-based oil and gas exploration company prior to joining Trinity.

In January 1999, Trinity scored a coup when John Adams, former CEO of Chase Bank of Texas, moved from Trinity's board of directors to become executive vice president of Trinity. As CEO of Chase, Adams knew Trinity's strength and reputation as a manufacturer within its industries. He wanted to see Trinity recognized as a diversified industrial company focused on growth. He fit in well and immediately started visiting with potential investors. "Today, there are so many alternatives for investors that if you don't visit with them regularly, communicate and share information about the strategic plan of the company, they'll find other investment options," Adams explained.

"Part of our strategy to improve shareholder value is for Tim and me to visit more regularly with the investment community. That means traveling to more cities, sitting down with more investor groups, attending more investor conferences and expand-ing the number of 'sell-side' analysts."[40]

Maintaining and improving that entrepre-neurial culture was Tim Wallace's principal goal. "That's what the whole organizational structure is geared towards," Wallace explained.

"We've created cross-functional teams that are tied in with a particular business unit to where they can operate the way an entrepreneur does in

a business. When an opportunity comes into play, we don't tie the hands of our people just because they have a budget already set. For instance, we don't say, 'Sorry, you don't have the money for that. Wait until next year.' We look at where the opportunity is, and then we assess the strengths of the benefits associated with it, and we'll make a quick decision."[41]

To this end, Wallace structured Trinity into three groups: the business group, focused on providing the best use of capital and generating profit; the shared service group, focused on identifying opportunities to improve efficiency and establish common business processes across the organization; and the corporate group, which provided overall governance, managed the com-pany's growth and developed strategies.

Wallace also introduced a four-point strategic planning process, which included a plan to address existing businesses; global expansion; new businesses/products/services; and business-to-business e-commerce.

To carry out his vision for blending e-commerce growth opportunities with Trinity's more tradi-tional markets, Wallace hired R. Stephen Polley, an accomplished Internet executive with over 25 years of experience in the high-tech industry. Wallace was attracted to Polley because of his track record for successfully creating and launch-ing Internet businesses. Polley joined Trinity from Cozone.com, where he was chairman and CEO. Polley is group president of Trinity e-Ventures, Inc., a wholly owned subsidiary established to build separate, independent companies to serve diversified industrial markets.

The key to Trinity's success ultimately depends on human resource skills. "People have various skills," explained Wallace.

"Some are good at keeping a business running. Some are good at turnaround and others are better at startups. Some are good at a variety of these, and what we are doing is establishing a way to evaluate our executives to see where we can best deploy them."[42]

Rounding out the executive suite to focus on the people side of the business, Wallace brought in

Mike Lintner, a seasoned executive who spent most of his career with IBM. "One of Wallace's goals was to make Trinity Industries one of the top places to work," said Lintner.

"Trinity has a legacy of being employee-focused and dedicated to its workforce. I am simply continuing that tradition with the development of a number of programs that include succession and career path planning, training and education modules."[43]

In 1999, Tim Wallace said that with the leadership team in place and a strategic planning process introduced, Trinity is prepared for the future. In five years, in addition to continuing to be the premier provider of products and services in their market sectors, Trinity will also be regarded as a leader in human resources.

"You'll see that we'll be well recognized for our state-of-the-art human resource strategies and programs in what we do, being able to evaluate the strengths that someone has and then placing him or her within our business. I want passionate workers. I am convinced that a passionate workplace will way outperform a partially motivated workplace."[44]

With 17,500 employees, Tim Wallace and his management team are poised for even greater accomplishments in the new millennium by building upon the success of the past. The 1999 annual report paid tribute to W. Ray Wallace, who laid the foundation for the company's success.

"The massive industrial power that Trinity Industries embodies today is a living tribute to the dedication, strategic vision, tenacity and integrity of W. Ray Wallace.... We will forever be in awe of the

In 1999, Tim Wallace succeeded his father, Ray Wallace, as Trinity's chairman and chief executive officer. The younger Wallace intends to double the size of Trinity in the new millennium.

mastery that Ray Wallace demonstrated in inspiring every employee of this company to achieve excellence and in confidently guiding Trinity from its beginnings as a youthful industry novice to become a major player in our markets."[45]

Notes to Sources

Chapter One

1. Ray Wallace, interviewed by the author, Sept. 15, 1998. Transcript, pp. 29-30.
2. Ray Wallace, interviewed by the author, Sept. 15, 1998. Transcript, pp. 29-30.
3. Ray Wallace, interviewed by the author, Sept. 15, 1998. Transcript, pp. 29-30.
4. "Report of Examination," Trinity Steel Company, Ltd. (A Partnership) Oct. 31, 1944.
5. Ray Wallace, interviewed by the author, Sept. 15, 1998. Transcript, p. 15.
6. Ray Wallace, interviewed by the author, Sept. 15, 1998. Transcript, p. 16.
7. "Report of Examination," Trinity Steel Company, Dec. 31, 1946.
8. Ray Wallace, interviewed by the author, Sept. 15, 1998. Transcript, p. 16.
9. "Trinity Steel of Dallas Adds Propane Equipment To Its Line," *Who's Who and What's What in the LP Gas Industry*, Feb. 1947: p. 3.
10. Tim Wallace, interviewed by the author, Oct. 28, 1998. Transcript, p. 10.
11. Dick Martin, interviewed by the author, Oct. 28, 1998. Transcript, p. 29.
12. Ray Wallace, interviewed by the author, Sept. 15, 1998. Transcript, pp. 27-28.
13. Ray Wallace, interviewed by the author, Sept. 15, 1998. Transcript, pp. 27-28.
14. Ray Wallace, interviewed by the author, Sept. 15, 1998. Transcript, pp. 27-28.
15. Ray Wallace, interviewed by the author, Sept. 15, 1998. Transcript, p. 28.
16. Tim Wallace, interviewed by the author, Oct. 28, 1998. Transcript, pp. 11-12.
17. Tim Wallace, interviewed by the author, Oct. 28, 1998. Transcript, p. 12.
18. Tim Wallace, interviewed by the author, Oct. 28, 1998. Transcript, p. 12.
19. Ray Wallace, interviewed by the author, Oct. 28, 1998. Transcript, p. 14.
20. *History of Texas, Together With a Biographical History of Tarrant and Parker Counties* (Chicago: The Lewis Publishing Co., 1895), p. 257.
21. *History of Texas, Together With a Biographical History of Tarrant and Parker Counties* (Chicago: The Lewis Publishing Co., 1895), p. 257.
22. Ray Wallace, interviewed by the author, Sept. 15, 1998. Transcript, pp. 2-3.
23. Tim Wallace, interviewed by the author, Oct. 28, 1998. Transcript, p. 11.
24. Ray Wallace, interviewed by the author, Sept. 15, 1998. Transcript, p. 12.
25. Ray Wallace, interviewed by the author, Sept. 15, 1998. Transcript, p. 13.
26. Ray Wallace, interviewed by the author, Sept. 15, 1998. Transcript, p. 17.
27. Ray Wallace, interviewed by the author, Sept. 15, 1998. Transcript, p. 16.
28. Andy Dworkin, "Passing the Torch: Trinity CEO to Step Down After 52-year Tenure, Son to Take Leadership of Industrial Products Firm," *Dallas Morning News*, July 18, 1998, p. 2F.
29. Ray Wallace, interviewed by the author, Sept. 15, 1998. Transcript, p. 18.
30. Ray Wallace, interviewed by the author, Sept. 15, 1998. Transcript, p. 18.
31. "Trinity Steel of Dallas Adds Propane Equipment To Its Line," *Who's Who and What's What in the LP Gas Industry*, Feb. 1947, p. 3.
32. Ray Wallace, interviewed by the author, Sept. 15, 1998. Transcript, p. 26.
33. Ray Wallace, interviewed by the author, Sept. 15, 1998. Transcript, p. 28.
34. Ray Wallace, interviewed by the author, Sept. 15, 1998. Transcript, p. 28.
35. Ray Wallace, interviewed by the author, Oct. 28, 1998. Transcript, p. 3.
36. "Profit and Loss Statement," Report of Examination, Trinity Steel Company (A Partnership) June 30, 1947, p. 12.
37. "Trinity Steel Facilities Expanded During Last Year," *Dallas Morning News*, Jan. 18, 1953, p. 16.
38. Trinity Steel Co., Inc., documents filed in the office of the Texas Secretary of State, Oct. 18, 1948.
39. Trinity Steel Co., Inc., documents filed in the office of the Texas Secretary of State, Oct. 18, 1948.

40. "Letter of Comments," Report of Examination: Trinity Steel Co., Inc., June 30, 1949, p. 2.
41. "Trinity Steel Opens," *Dallas* magazine, July 1957, p. 62.
42. Report of Examination: Trinity Steel Co., Inc., June 30, 1951, p. 3.
43. "Trinity Steel Facilities Expanded During Last Year," *Dallas Morning News,* Jan. 18, 1953, p. 16.
44. "Trinity Steel Facilities Expanded During Last Year," *Dallas Morning News,* Jan. 18, 1953: 10:16.
45. "Letter of Comments," Report of Examination: Wallace-Johnson, July 31, 1953, p. 2.
46. Report of Examination: Wallace-Johnson, July 31, 1953, p. 3.
47. "Construction Planned by Trinity Steel," *Dallas* magazine, July 1955, p. 31.
48. Letter to the Stockholders, Trinity Steel Company, Inc., Annual Report, 1958.
49. Ray Wallace, interviewed by the author, Sept. 15, 1998. Transcript, p. 22.

Chapter One Sidebar

1. "The First Fifty Years of LP-Gas: An Industry Chronology," *LPGA Times,* Jan.-Sept. 1962, "Chapter 2: Pioneer Installations Are Made," *LPGA Times,* Feb. 1962, p. 22.
2. Ronald E. Cannon, *The Gas Processing Industry: Origins and Evolution* (Tulsa, Okla.: Gas Processors Association, 1993), p. 216.
3. "The First Fifty Years of LP-Gas: An Industry Chronology," *LPGA Times,*

Jan.-Sept. 1962, "Chapter 1: The Dream of LP-Gas Becomes Reality," *LPGA Times,* Jan. 1962, p. 17.
4. Ronald E. Cannon, *The Gas Processing Industry: Origins & Evolution* (Tulsa, Okla.: Gas Processors Association, 1993), p. 216.
5. "The First Fifty Years of LP-Gas: An Industry Chronology," *LPGA Times,* Jan.-Sept. 1962, "Chapter 4: 'Big Names' Rally to LP-Gas," *LPGA Times,* April 1962, p. 18.
6. "The First Fifty Years of LP-Gas: An Industry Chronology," *LPGA Times,* Jan.-Sept. 1962, "Chapter 4: 'Big Names' Rally to LP-Gas," *LPGA Times,* April 1962, p. 21.

Chapter Two

1. Ed Boulter, interviewed by Joan Thompson, March 24, 1999. Transcript, p. 14.
2. Ralph Banks, interviewed by the author, Oct. 28, 1998. Transcript, p. 6.
3. "Directors' Meeting," Meetings of Directors of Dallas Tank Co., Inc., Oct. 27, 1933, through March 8, 1950, Oct. 27, 1933.
4. Evelyn Miller Crowell, ed., *Men of Achievement,* Texas ed. (Dallas: John Moranz Associates, 1948), p. 120.
5. "William W. Banks," *Dallas Times Herald,* Nov. 18, 1982, p. D7.
6. Evelyn Miller Crowell, ed., *Men of Achievement,* Texas ed. (Dallas: John Moranz Associates, 1948), p. 120.
7. Sue Gibbons, interviewed by Joan Thompson, Feb. 3, 1999. Transcript, p. 4.

8. "Special Stockholders' Meeting," Meetings of the Stockholders of Dallas Tank Co. Inc., Oct. 25, 1933, through Mar. 28, 1958, Dec. 20, 1939.
9. "Oil Well Supplies ... Keep Many Wheels Turning," *Dallas* magazine, Jan. 1940, pp. 60-61.
10. Prospectus: 150,000 Shares, Trinity Steel Company, Inc., Common Stock (Par Value $1.00) (Eppler, Guerin & Turner, Inc., 1964), p. 7.
11. "William W. Banks," *Dallas Times Herald,* Nov. 18, 1982, p. D7.
12. Ralph Banks, interviewed by the author, Oct. 28, 1998. Transcript, p. 1.
13. Ralph Banks, interviewed by the author, Oct. 28, 1998. Transcript, p. 1.
14. Ralph Banks, interviewed by the author, Oct. 28, 1998. Transcript, p. 3.
15. Ralph Banks, interviewed by the author, Oct. 28, 1998. Transcript, p. 4.
16. "Special Directors' Meeting," Meetings of Directors of Dallas Tank Co., Inc., Oct. 27, 1933, through March 8, 1950, Jun. 19, 1944.
17. Prospectus: 150,000 Shares, Trinity Steel Company, Inc., Common Stock (Par Value $1.00) (Eppler, Guerin & Turner, Inc., 1964), p. 7.
18. Evelyn Miller Crowell, ed., *Men of Achievement,* Texas ed. (Dallas: John Moranz Associates, 1948), p. 120.
19. Evelyn Miller Crowell, ed., *Men of Achievement,* Texas ed. (Dallas: John Moranz Associates, 1948), p. 120.

20. Evelyn Miller Crowell, ed., *Men of Achievement,* Texas ed. (Dallas: John Moranz Associates, 1948), p. 120. John Banks, interviewed by Joan Thompson, Feb. 24, 1999. Transcript, p. 11.

21. Evelyn Miller Crowell, ed., *Men of Achievement,* Texas ed. (Dallas: John Moranz Associates, 1948), p. 120.

22. "Home Industry: Dallas Tank Company," *Dallas* magazine, Oct. 1948, p. 10.

23. "Home Industry: Dallas Tank Company," *Dallas* magazine, Oct. 1948, p. 15.

24. "Minutes of Annual Stockholders Meeting of Dallas Tank Company," Meetings of the Stockholders of Dallas Tank Co., Inc., Oct. 25, 1933, through March 28, 1958, Jan. 27, 1953.

25. "Minutes of Annual Stockholders Meeting of Dallas Tank Company," Meetings of the Stockholders of Dallas Tank Co., Inc., Oct. 25, 1933, through March 28, 1958, Jan. 27, 1953.

26. "Financial Position, Vicksburg Tank Company," documents filed with the Texas Secretary of State Office, April 1, 1955.

27. "Minutes of Special Meeting of Directors Held on March 3, 1958," Dallas Tank Company, Inc., Mar. 3, 1958.

28. "Annual Meeting of Stockholders," Meetings of the Stockholders of Dallas Tank Co., Inc., Oct. 25, 1933, through March 28, 1958, Jan. 26, 1954.

29. "Annual Meeting of Stockholders," Meetings of the Stockholders of Dallas Tank Co., Inc., Oct. 25, 1933, through March 28, 1958, Jan. 26, 1954.

30. Ralph Banks, interviewed by the author, Oct. 28, 1998. Transcript, p. 14.

31. "Statement of Income and Earned Surplus, Dallas Tank Company, Inc., Years Ended Dec. 31, 1954, and Dec. 31, 1953," filed with the Texas Secretary of State, Mar. 2, 1955.

32. "Resolution," Meetings of Directors of Dallas Tank Co., Inc., Jan. 2, 1951, through Aug. 5, 1957, July 26, 1955.

33. "Regular Directors Meeting," Meetings of Directors of Dallas Tank Co., Inc., Jan. 2, 1951, through Aug. 5, 1957, April 26, 1957.

34. Ray Wallace, interviewed by the author, Oct. 28, 1998. Transcript, pp. 5-6.

35 "Charles Sammons, 90, Executive," *The New York Times,* November 14, 1988, p. D13.

36. Jess T. Hay, interviewed by Joan Thompson, Feb. 2, 1999. Transcript, p. 5.

37. "Minutes of Special Meeting of Directors Held on March 3, 1958," Dallas Tank Company, Inc., Mar. 3, 1958.

38. "Minutes of Special Meeting of Directors Held on Sept. 9, 1958," Dallas Tank Co., Inc., Sept. 9, 1958.

39. "Minutes of Special Meeting of Directors Held on Sept. 9, 1958," Dallas Tank Co., Inc., Sept. 9, 1958.

40. Jeff Walls, assistant controller, "Trinity Industries, Inc., Supplemental Information," undated.

Chapter Two Sidebar

1. Frank X. Tolbert, "Tolbert's Texas: Brother Bill Harrod 'Worked His Heart Out,'" *Dallas Morning News,* April 8, 1976.

2. Kenneth Force, "Promise Led Him Near Starvation," *Dallas Morning News,* Nov. 26, 1950.

3. Kenneth Force, "Promise Led Him Near Starvation," *Dallas Morning News,* Nov. 26, 1950.

4. Juanita Bailey, interviewed by Alex Lieber, August 31, 1999.

5. Kenneth Force, "Promise Led Him Near Starvation," *Dallas Morning News,* Nov. 26, 1950.

Chapter Three

1. Ralph Banks, interviewed by the author, Oct. 28, 1999. Transcript, p. 11.

2. Obituary, "Charles Sammons, 90, Executive," *The New York Times,* November 14, 1988, p. D13.

3. 1958 Annual Report.

4. Dick Martin, interviewed by the author, Oct. 28, 1998. Transcript, p. 4.

5. Edmund Hoffman, interviewed by Joan Thompson, Jan. 6, 1999. Transcript, p. 14.

6. Ralph Banks, interviewed by the author, Oct. 28, 1998. Transcript, p. 10.

7. Ralph Banks, interviewed by the author, Oct. 28, 1999. Transcript, p. 9.

8. Ralph Banks, interviewed by the author, Oct. 28, 1999. Transcript, p. 10.

9. Ralph Banks, interviewed by the author, Oct. 28, 1999. Transcript, p. 10.

10. Ralph Banks, interviewed by the author, Oct. 28, 1999. Transcript, p. 9.

11. Ralph Banks, interviewed by the author, Oct. 28, 1999. Transcript, p. 11.

12. Ralph Banks, interviewed by the author, Oct. 28, 1998. Transcript, p. 10.

13. Jess Hay, interviewed by Joan Thompson, Feb. 2, 1999. Transcript, p. 11.

14. "Road," Microsoft Encarta 97 Encyclopedia (Microsoft Corporation), 1993-1996.

15. Ray Wallace, interviewed by the author, Oct. 28, 1998. Transcript, p. 9.

16. C.J. Bender, letter to stockholders, Trinity Steel Company, Inc., Annual Report for the year ended Mar. 31, 1960.

17. C.J. Bender, letter to stockholders, Trinity Steel Company, Inc., Annual Report for the year ended Mar. 31, 1960.

18. C.J. Bender, letter to stockholders, Trinity Steel Company, Inc., Annual Report for the year ended Dec. 31, 1958.

19. Jim Stephenson, "Young Men Going Places: Ray Wallace," *Dallas* magazine, Dec. 1959, p. 48.

Chapter Four

1. Ralph Banks, interviewed by the author, Oct. 28, 1998. Transcript, p. 23.

2. Ray Wallace, interviewed by the author, Oct. 28, 1998. Transcript, p. 12.

3. Ray Wallace, interviewed by the author, Oct. 28, 1998, transcript, pp. 20-21.

4. Tim Wallace, interviewed by the author, Oct. 28, 1998. Transcript, p. 18.

5. Jess T. Hay, interviewed by Joan Thompson, Feb. 2, 1999. Transcript, p. 5.

6. "Minutes of the Quarterly Meeting of the Board of Directors, Sept. 25, 1961," Trinity Steel Company, Inc. (Formerly: Dallas Tank Company, Inc.), vol. 3.

7. Ralph Banks, interviewed by the author, Oct. 28, 1998. Transcript, p. 23.

8. Lee McElroy, interviewed by Joan Thompson, Feb. 10, 1999. Transcript, p. 2.

9. Lee McElroy, interviewed by Joan Thompson, Feb. 10, 1999. Transcript, p. 4.

10. Lee McElroy, interviewed by Joan Thompson, Feb. 10, 1999. Transcript, pp. 2-3.

11. "Minutes of the Quarterly Meeting of the Board of Directors, Sept. 25, 1961," Trinity Steel Company, Inc. (Formerly Dallas Tank Company, Inc.), vol. 3.

12. "Dallas Steel Firm Buying Tulsa Plant," *Tulsa World,* Nov. 29, 1961.

13. Epplin, Guerin & Turner, Inc., representatives of the underwriters, 150,000 Shares, Trinity Steel Co., Inc., Common Stock (Par Value $1.00), Prospectus, Aug. 13, 1964, p. 7.

14. Ralph Banks, interviewed by the author, Oct. 28, 1998. Transcript, p. 23.

15. Ralph Banks, interviewed by the author, Oct. 28, 1998. Transcript, p. 24.

16. Edmund Hoffman, interviewed by Joan Thompson, Jan. 6, 1999. Transcript, p. 20.

17. Dick Martin, interviewed by the author, Oct. 28, 1998. Transcript, p. 5.

18. Dick Martin, interviewed by the author, Oct. 28, 1998. Transcript, p. 6.

19. Philip Van Munching, *Beer Blast* (Random House, Inc., New York), 1997: p. 28. This interesting and balanced book focuses on the marketing battles in the beer industry rather than on a technical history of brewing.

20. Epplin, Guerin & Turner, Inc., representatives of the underwriters, Trinity Steel Company, Inc., $2,500,000 Principal Amount 5 1/2% Convertible Subordinated Debentures Due Feb. 15, 1981, Prospectus, Feb. 8, 1966, p. 11.

21. Epplin, Guerin & Turner, Inc., representatives of the underwriters, Trinity Steel Company, Inc., $2,500,000 Principal Amount 5 1/2% Convertible Subordinated Debentures Due Feb. 15, 1981, Prospectus, Feb. 8, 1966, pp. 12-13.

22. Darwin Payne, *Dallas: An Illustrated History* (Woodland Hills, Calif: Windsor Publications, Inc., 1982), p. 375.

23. "Minutes of the Annual Meeting of the Board of Directors Held on June 17, 1964," Trinity Steel Company, Inc. (Formerly: Dallas Tank Company, Inc.), vol. 4, p. 7.

24. "Trinity Steel Sets Dividend," *Dallas Morning News,* July 1, 1964, p. 2.8.

25. Ray Wallace, interviewed by the author, July 13, 1999. Transcript, p. 4.
26. Epplin, Guerin & Turner, Inc., representatives of the underwriters, Trinity Steel Company, Inc., $2,500,000 Principal Amount 5 1/2% Convertible Subordinated Debentures Due Feb. 15, 1981, Prospectus, Feb. 8, 1966, p. 21.
27. "To Our Stockholders," Trinity Steel Company, Inc., Annual Report, 1964.
28. Jess T. Hay, interviewed by Joan Thompson, Feb. 2, 1999. Transcript, p. 14.
29. "To Our Stockholders," Trinity Steel Company, Inc., Annual Report, 1965, p. 5.

Chapter Five

1. Ray Wallace, interviewed by the author, Oct. 28, 1998. Transcript, p. 14.
2. Ralph Banks, interviewed by the author, Oct. 28, 1998. Transcript, p. 13.
3. Ralph Banks, interviewed by the author, Oct. 28, 1998. Transcript, p. 13.
4. Buddy Alexander, interviewed by David Patten, June 24, 1999. Transcript, p. 8.
5. Ray Wallace, interviewed by the author, Oct. 28, 1998. Transcript, p. 14.
6. "Minutes of Meeting of the Board of Directors Held May 25, 1966," Trinity Industries, Inc. (formerly: Trinity Steel Company, Inc.), vol. 6, p. 2.
7. "The Year in Review," Trinity Industries, Inc., Annual Report, 1968, p. 7.
8. Lee McElroy, interviewed by Joan Thompson, Feb. 10, 1999. Transcript, p. 17.

9. "To Our Stockholders," Trinity Industries, Inc., Annual Report, 1967, p. 5.
10. "To Our Stockholders," Trinity Industries, Inc., Annual Report, 1967, p. 5.
11. "To Our Stockholders," Trinity Industries, Inc., Annual Report, 1967, p. 5.
12. "Minutes of Regular Meeting of Board of Directors Held on December 19, 1966," Trinity Industries, Inc. (Formerly: Trinity Steel Company, Inc.), vol. 7, p. 1.
13. "Review of Operations," Trinity Industries, Inc., Annual Report, 1967, p. 8.
14. Don Hestand, interviewed by David Patten, June 24, 1999. Transcript, p. 15.
15. Don Hestand, interviewed by David Patten, June 24, 1999. Transcript, p. 16.
16. Don Hestand, interviewed by David Patten, June 24, 1999. Transcript, p. 16.
17. Don Graham, interviewed by the author, Oct. 28, 1998. Transcript, p. 2.
18. Don Graham, interviewed by the author, Oct. 28, 1998. Transcript, p. 3.
19. Don Graham, interviewed by the author, Oct. 28, 1998. Transcript, pp. 4-5.
20. Trinity Industries, Inc., Annual Report, 1971.
21. Don Hestand, interviewed by David Patten, June 24, 1999. Transcript, p. 5.
22. Trinity Industries, Inc., Annual Report, 1970.
23. Trinity Industries, Inc., Annual Report, 1970.
24. Don Hestand, interviewed by David Patten, June 24, 1999. Transcript, p. 7.
25. Dick Martin, interviewed by Alex Lieber, July 22, 1999, in a telephone conversation. No transcript. Besides his two formal interviews, Mr. Martin kindly answered questions as they came up during the research.
26. Don Graham, interviewed by Alex Lieber, July 23, 1999. Transcript, p. 24.
27. "Trinity Industries Buys Amarillo Machine Firm," *Dallas Times Herald,* Dec. 20, 1968.
28. "The Year in Review," Trinity Industries, Inc., Annual Report, 1969, p. 5.
29. "Listing Application to New York Stock Exchange, Inc.," Trinity Industries, Inc., Mar. 31, 1972, p. 5.
30. "Message from the Chairman and President," Trinity Industries, Inc., Annual Report, 1970.
31. "Message from the Chairman and President," Trinity Industries, Inc., Annual Report, 1970.

Chapter Five Sidebar

1 "Transportation," Encyclopedia Brittanica, Vol. 28 (Macropædia, 1996).
2. George Brown Tindall and David Emory Shi, *America* (W.W. Norton & Co., New York, 1997), pp. 336-338.
3. *Encyclopedia of North American Railroading: 150 Years of Railroading in the U.S. and Canada,* ed. Freeman Hubbard (New York: McGraw-Hill Book Co., 1981), p. 244.
4. George Brown Tindall and David Emory Shi, *America* (New York: W.W. Norton & Co.,1997), pp. 336-338.

5. Marchia D. Lowe, *Back on Track: The Global Rail Revival*, ed. Carole Douglis, Worldwatch Pater 118 (Washington D.C.: Worldwatch Institute, 1994), p. 20.
6. Robert C. Lieb, *Transportation*, 3rd ed. (Reston, Va.: Reston Publishing Co., 1985), p. 9.

Chapter Six

1. "Message from the Chairman and President To Our Stockholders," Trinity Industries, Inc., Annual Report, 1971.
2. "Trinity Industries Announces New Process Division Established in Tulsa," *Tulsa World*, July 22, 1970.
3. Christopher G. L. Hall, *Steel Phoenix: The Fall and Rise of the U.S. Steel Industry* (New York: St. Martin's Press, 1997), p. 81.
4. Don Graham, interviewed by the author, Oct. 28, 1998. Transcript, p. 13.
5. Rube Perrin, interviewed by David Patten, August 13, 1999. Transcript, p. 9.
6. Rube Perrin, interviewed by David Patten, August 13, 1999. Transcript, p. 15.
7. "Message from the Chairman and President," Trinity Industries, Inc., Annual Report, 1970.
8. "Message from the Chairman and President," Trinity Industries, Inc., Annual Report, 1970.
9. Bill Reed, "At Trinity, Production Outweighs the Glamor," *Dallas Times Herald*, July 23, 1972.
10. Bill Reed, "At Trinity, Production Outweighs the Glamor," *Dallas Times Herald*, July 23, 1972.
11. Bill Reed, "At Trinity, Production Outweighs the Glamor," *Dallas Times Herald*, July 23, 1972.
12. "Message from the Chairman and President To Our Stockholders," Trinity Industries, Inc., Annual Report, 1971.
13. "Stockholder Meeting Briefs," *The Wall Street Journal*, July 13, 1972, p. 32.
14. Jack Cunningham, interviewed by the author, July 13, 1999. Transcript, p. 4.
15. Oscar Stewart, interviewed by Joan Thompson, July 13, 1999. Transcript, p. 27.
16. Jack Cunningham, interviewed by the author, July 13, 1999. Transcript, p. 5.
17. "Acquisitions," Trinity Industries Inc., Annual Report 1973, p. 22.
18. "Patriot of Year Is Neville Levy," New Orleans *Times-Picayune*, Feb. 23, 1973.
19. Allen Johnson, "Equitable Builds Cementing Barge," *Industrial Weekly* of the *New Orleans Item*, May 3, 1954, p. 1.
20. John Pope, "America's Ship Came In With Help From Higgins," New Orleans *Times-Picayune*, May 5, 1985, p. A21.
21. John Pope, "America's Ship Came In With Help From Higgins," New Orleans *Times-Picayune*, May 5, 1985, p. A21.
22. John Pope, "America's Ship Came In With Help From Higgins," New Orleans *Times-Picayune*, May 5, 1985, p. A21.
23. John Pope, "America's Ship Came In With Help From Higgins," New Orleans *Times-Picayune*, May 5, 1985, p. A21.
24. Mark Magnier, "LASH Ship Concept Never Quite Lived Up to its Early Billing," *Journal of Commerce*, May 17, 1990. Maritime section, p. 1B.
25. Donald F. Wood and James C. Johnson, *Contemporary Transportation*, The PennWell Marketing and Management Series (Tulsa: PennWell Publishing Co., 1983), p. 331.
26. The Mosher Steel Company, 75th Anniversary, pamphlet, published about 1960, p. 3.
27. The Mosher Steel Company, 75th Anniversary, pamphlet, published about 1960, p. 3.
28. Evelyn Miller Crowell, ed., "William Stephen Mosher, A Memorial," *Men of Achievement*, Texas ed. (Dallas: John Moranz Associates, 1948), p. 122.
29. The Mosher Steel Company, 75th Anniversary, pamphlet, published about 1960, p. 4.
30. Al Altwegg, "For More Than 80 Years, Mosher Builds Dallas," *Dallas Morning News*, Mar. 13, 1956.
31. Ken Lewis, interviewed by Alex Lieber, February 1, 2000. Taped interview.
32. Jack Cunningham, interviewed by the author, July 13, 1999. Transcript, p. 9.

33. "To Our Shareholders,"
Trinity Industries Inc.,
Annual Report, 1974, p. 3.
34. "To Our Shareholders,"
Trinity Industries, Inc.,
Annual Report, 1974, p. 3.
35. "Hopper Shortage Puts
Squeeze on Shippers,"
Chemical Week, Feb. 22,
1978, p. 38.
36. Walter Isaacson, *Kissinger,
A Biography* (New York:
Touchstone, 1996), p. 428.
37. "Containers," Trinity
Industries, Inc., Annual
Report, 1973, p. 7.

Chapter Six Sidebar

1. Retired Navy Capt. Thomas
L. Lewis, "Matters Marine:
Shipbuilder Recognized for
Offshore Oil, Gas Work,"
New Orleans *Times-
Picayune* Jan. 7, 1973,
p. 1.38.
2. "Gamble in the Gulf," *Kermac
News*, Dec. 1972, p. 4.
3. "Gamble in the Gulf," *Kermac
News*, Dec. 1972, p. 6.

Chapter Seven

1. Ray Wallace, interviewed by
the author, Oct. 28, 1998.
Transcript, p. 16.
2. "Behind Trinity Industries'
Explosion: Prosaic Metal
Fabricator's Stock
Quadruples in '75,"
Financial World, Oct. 29,
1975, p. 31.
3. "Behind Trinity Industries'
Explosion: Prosaic Metal
Fabricator's Stock
Quadruples in '75,"
Financial World, Oct. 29,
1975, p. 31.
4. Don Hestand, interviewed by
David Patten, June 24,
1999. Transcript, p. 24.

5. Ed Boulter, interviewed by
Joan Thompson, March 24,
1999. Transcript, p. 19.
6. Jean A. Briggs, "What to
look for in a tax shelter,"
Forbes, September 17,
1979, p. 70.
7. Ray Wallace, interviewed by
the author, Oct. 28, 1998.
Transcript, p. 14.
8. Ray Wallace, interviewed by
the author, Oct. 28, 1998.
Transcript, p. 15.
9. Dick Martin, interviewed by
the author, Oct. 28, 1998.
Transcript, pp. 11-12.
10. Steve Smith, interviewed by
the author, July 13, 1999.
Transcript, pp. 6-7.
11. Steve Smith, interviewed by
the author, July 13, 1999.
Transcript, p. 12.
12. Ray Wallace, interviewed by
the author, Oct. 28, 1998.
Transcript, p. 16.
13. Mitchell Gordon, "Huge
Backlog Helps Bolster
Outlook at Trinity
Industries," *Barron's*, Feb.
24, 1974, p. 35.
14. "Trinity Industries Sets
Sights On Seventh Straight
Peak Year," *Barron's*, Dec.
12, 1977, rpt. as Dow
Jones Reprint Service,
1977.
15. "Trinity Plans Expansion,"
*The Longview News
Journal*, Mar. 25, 1979,
p. 7B.
16. "Minutes of Regular
Meeting of Board of
Directors," Trinity
Industries, Inc. (Formerly:
Trinity Steel Company,
Inc.), vol. 10, Dec. 9, 1976,
p. 5.
17. "Railcar Newcomer: Trinity
Industries' Timely
Expansion Could Mean
$2.50 For Fiscal 1980,"

Barron's, Oct. 15, 1979,
p. 44.
18. "Segment Information,"
Trinity Industries, Inc.
Annual Report 1980, p. 25.
19. Ibid.
20. Steve Smith, interviewed by
the author, July 13, 1999.
Transcript, p. 37.
21. Steve Smith, interviewed by
the author, July 13, 1999.
Transcript, p. 37.
22. Richard Brown, interviewed
by Alex Lieber, June 16,
1999. Transcript, p. 3.
23. Richard Brown, interviewed
by Alex Lieber, June 16,
1999. Transcript, p. 3.
24. "Railcars," Trinity
Industries, Inc., Annual
Report 1980, p. 6.
25. "To Our Shareholders,"
Trinity Industries, Inc.
Annual Report 1980, p. 2.
26. "C.J. Bender: 1889-1977,"
Trinity Industries, Inc.
Annual Report 1977, p. 20.
27. Lee McElroy, interviewed
by Joan Thompson, Feb.
10, 1999. Transcript, p. 19.
28. "Minutes of the Annual
Meeting of Shareholders,"
Trinity Industries, Inc.
(Formerly: Trinity Steel
Company, Inc.), vol. 10,
July 13, 1977, p. 4.
29. "Railcars," Trinity
Industries, Inc. Annual
Report 1980, p. 6.

Chapter Eight

1. Tim Wallace, interviewed by
the author, October 28,
1998. Transcript,0. p. 22.
2. Don Graham, interviewed by
Alex Lieber, July 23, 1999.
Transcript, p. 3.
3. "First U.S. Ferry Equipped
With Cycloidal Propellers
Set For Service Debut,"

Maritime Reporter/ Engineering News, September 1, 1981, p. 18.

4. "First U.S. Ferry Equipped With Cycloidal Propellers Set For Service Debut," *Maritime Reporter/ Engineering News,* September 1, 1981, p. 18.

5. Tim Wallace, interviewed by the author, Oct. 28, 1998. Transcript, p. 24.

6. Don Graham, interviewed by Alex Lieber, July 23, 1999. Transcript, p. 7.

7. Don Graham, interviewed by Alex Lieber, July 23, 1999. Transcript, p. 7.

8. Don Graham, interviewed by Alex Lieber, July 23, 1999. Transcript, p. 7.

9. "Operations Review: Marine Products," Trinity Industries, Inc. Annual Report 1981, p. 10.

10. John Hall, "Trinity Industries Inc. Purchases Gretna Firm," New Orleans *Times-Picayune,* Feb. 3, 1981, p. 2.10.

11. "Annual Meeting of Shareholders," Trinity Industries Inc. (Formerly Trinity Steel Company, Inc.), vol. 12, July 16, 1980, p. 4.

12. "Annual Meeting of Shareholders," Trinity Industries Inc. (Formerly Trinity Steel Company, Inc.), vol. 12, July 16, 1980, pp. 4-5.

13. Rotan Mosle Inc., Trinity Industries, Inc., report, Mar. 4, 1983, p. 7.

14. "Minutes of Regular Meeting of Board of Directors," Trinity Industries Inc. (Formerly: Trinity Steel Company, Inc.), vol. 12, Sept. 11, 1980, p. 4.

15. "To Our Shareholders," Trinity Industries, Inc., Annual Report 1981, p. 3.

16. R. Lee Sullivan, "Nobody Else Wanted Them," *Forbes,* Oct. 10, 1994, p. 58.

17. Rotan Mosle Inc., Trinity Industries, Inc., report, Mar. 4, 1983, p. 7.

18. $275,000,000 Trinity Industries, Inc. Liquid Yield Option Notes Due 2001, Prospectus, Feb. 14, 1986, p. 8.

19. Tim Wallace, interviewed by the author, Oct. 28, 1998. Transcript, p. 34.

20. Kerry Hannon, "Closely Watched Trainmaker," *Forbes,* April 2, 1990, p. 204.

21. Keith Hittle, interviewed by Alex Lieber, July 8, 1999. Transcript, p. 3.

22. Donald F. Wood and James C. Johnson, *Contemporary Transportation,* 2nd ed., The PennWell Marketing and Management Series (Tulsa: PennWell Publishing Co., 1983), p. 184.

23. "Operations Review: Railcars," Trinity Industries, Inc. Annual Report, 1981, p. 4.

24. "Railcars," Trinity Industries, Inc. 1983 Annual Report, p. 6.

25. Tim Wallace, interviewed by the author, Oct. 28, 1998. Transcript, p. 30.

26. Warren Vieth, "Trinity Buys New Orleans Shipbuilding Firm," *Dallas Times-Herald,* Sept. 12, 1983, p. B3.

27. "Research and Development: Diesel Electric Propulsion," Halter Marine Inc.: The Total Shipbuilding Group, brochure, circa 1980, p. 28.

28. "Surface Effect Ships," Halter Marine Inc.: The Total Shipbuilding Group, brochure, circa 1980, p. 36.

29. "Major Projects Completed 1980 and Later," Trinity Industries, Inc., Structural Steel Division, list.

30. "McDermott Inc. to Sell Some of Unit's Assets to Trinity Industries Inc.," *The Wall Street Journal,* Sept. 1, 1981, p. 18.

31. "Business Acquisitions," Trinity Industries Inc., Annual Report 1984, p. 17.

32. Cecil Spear, interviewed by Alex Lieber, June 21, 1999. Transcript, p. 13.

33. Ray Wallace, interviewed by the author, Oct. 28, 1998. Transcript, p. 18.

34. "Pullman Pulls Out of Carbuilding, Sells to Trinity," *Railway Age,* Nov. 1983, p. 26.

35. "Railcars," Trinity Industries Inc. Annual Report 1984, p. 6.

36. Ken Lewis, interviewed by Alex Lieber, February 1, 2000. Taped interview.

37. "Suppliers Take a Bleak Tale to Congress," *Railway Age,* Nov. 1983, p. 26.

38. Herb Greenberg, "Pullman Switches Off Rail Cars," *Chicago Tribune,* Oct. 1, 1983, p. 2.7.

39. Trinity Industries Inc., news release, Sept. 30, 1983, pp. 1-2.

Chapter Eight Sidebar: Ingalls

1. "The Ingalls Story," The Ingalls Companies: Steel, Skill and Service, pamphlet, circa 1976, p. 2.

2. "The Ingalls Story," The Ingalls Companies: Steel,

Skill and Service, pamphlet, circa 1976, p. 3.

3. "The Ingalls Story," The Ingalls Companies: Steel, Skill and Service, pamphlet, circa 1978, p. 3.

4. Richard Austin Smith, "The Haunted House of Ingalls," *Fortune*, May 1958, p. 228.

5. Richard Austin Smith, "The Haunted House of Ingalls," *Fortune*, May 1958, pp. 228, 233.

6. Richard Austin Smith, "The Haunted House of Ingalls," *Fortune*, May 1958, p. 233.

7. "Family Feud," *Time*, Oct. 6, 1952, p. 94.

8. "Family Feud," *Time*, Oct. 6, 1952, p. 94.

Chapter Eight Sidebar: Halter Marine

1. Gil T. Webre, "Crewboat Contract Started Halter on Road to Boatbuilding Success," New Orleans *Times-Picayune*, Jan. 16, 1976, p. 3.1.

2. Gil T. Webre, "Crewboat Contract Started Halter on Road to Boatbuilding Success," New Orleans *Times-Picayune*, Jan. 16, 1976, p. 3.1.

3. "Supply Boats," Halter Marine Inc.: The Total Shipbuilding Group, brochure, circa 1980, p. 24.

4. Gil T. Webre, "Crewboat Contract Started Halter on Road to Boatbuilding Success," New Orleans *Times-Picayune*, Jan. 16, 1976, p. 3.1.

5. "John Hall, "Revenues Up 54% at Halter in 1980," New Orleans *Times-Picayune*, Jan. 21, 1981, p. 5.10.

6. John Hall, "Trinity Ups N.O. Stake With Halter Purchase," New Orleans *Times-Picayune*, Sept. 22, 1983, p. 2.10.

Chapter Nine

1. Liston Edgington Leyendecker, *Palace Car Prince: A Biography of George Mortimer Pullman* (Niwot, Colo.: U P of Colorado, 1992), p. 264.

2. Peter T. Maiken, *Night Trains: The Pullman System in the Golden Years of American Travel* (Baltimore: The Johns Hopkins UP, 1989), p. 8.

3. Liston Edgington Leyendecker, *Palace Car Prince: A Biography of George Mortimer Pullman* (Niwot, Colo.: UP of Colorado, 1992), p. 24.

4. Paul Ackerman, ed., "George M. Pullman Had an Idea ... and It Grew, and Grew, and Grew!," *The Carbuilder*, Mar. 1955, p. 4.

5. Joseph Husband, *The Story of the Pullman Car* (1917; New York: Arno Press, 1972), pp. 28-29.

6. Lucius Beebe, *Mr. Pullman's Elegant Palace Car* (Garden City, N.Y.: Doubleday, 1961), p. 138.

7. Joseph Husband, *The Story of the Pullman Car* (1917; New York: Arno Press, 1972), p. 47.

8. Joseph Husband, *The Story of the Pullman Car* (1917; New York: Arno Press, 1972), p. 49.

9. Charles M. Knoll, *Go Pullman* (Rochester, N.Y.: Rochester Chapter, National Railway Historical Society, 1995), p. 34.

10. Liston Edgington Leyendecker, *Palace Car Prince: A Biography of George Mortimer Pullman* (Niwot, Colo.: U P of Colorado, 1992), p. 264.

11. George H. Douglas, *All Aboard! The Railroad in American Life* (New York: Paragon House, 1992), p. 225.

12. Charles M. Knoll, *Go Pullman* (Rochester, N.Y.: Rochester Chapter, National Railway Historical Society, 1995), p. 49.

13. "Pullman Incorporated," *Fortune*, Jan. 1938, p. 94.

14. "Pullman in Big Merger," *The New York Times*, Oct. 22, 1921, p. 23.

15. "Heads Pullman Company," *The New York Times*, Jan. 17, 1922, p. 23.

16. Paul Ackerman, ed., "Michigan City's Haskell & Barker Plant, *The Carbuilder*, Mar. 1955, p. 13.

17. Paul Ackerman, ed., "Michigan City's Haskell & Barker Plant," *The Carbuilder*, Mar. 1955, p. 13.

18. "History of the Bessemer Plant," Trinity Industries, Inc., news release, Jan. 23, 1995, p. 1.

19. "Pullman Incorporated," *Fortune*, Jan. 1938, p. 94.

20. "Pullman Incorporated," *Fortune*, Jan. 1938, p. 94.

21. "Pullman Monopoly," *Time*, July 22, 1940, p. 72.

22. "Half Off for Cash," *Business Week*, Sept. 15, 1945, p. 54.

23. Paul Ackerman, ed., "The Butler Story: Two Men and

an Idea," *The Carbuilder,* Mar. 1955, p. 21.

24. Paul Ackerman, ed., "Bessemer, Alabama, Our Southern Plant," *The Carbuilder,* Mar. 1955, p. 30.

25. John F. Stover, *American Railroads,* 2nd ed. (Chicago: U of Chicago P, 1997), p. 218.

26. Charles W. Bryan Jr., "Future Planning Builds on History," ed. Paul Ackerman, *The Carbuilder,* Mar. 1955, p. 1.

27. "Rip Van Pullman," *Forbes,* May 1, 1966, p. 26.

28. "Rip Van Pullman," *Forbes,* May 1, 1966, p. 26.

29. "Freight-car Builders Hit Full Throttle," *Business Week,* July 16, 1966, p. 106.

30. "Rip Van Pullman," *Forbes,* May 1, 1966, p. 27.

31. Don Bodinger, interviewed by David Patten, June 17, 1999. Transcript, p. 14.

32. John R. Dorfman, "Bye-bye Boxcars," *Forbes,* June 7, 1982, p. 135.

33. "How a Fixed-Price Contract Derailed Pullman," *Business Week,* Mar. 17, 1975, p. 56.

34. Frank N. Wilner, *The Amtrak Story* (Omaha: Simmons-Boardman Books, 1994), p. 70.

35. David Young, "Spotlight: Few Caught Napping By Pullman Decision," Mar. 28, 1979, p. 4.1.

36. David Young, "Spotlight: Few Caught Napping By Pullman Decision," Mar. 28, 1979, p. 4.1.

37. "Rip Van Pullman," *Forbes,* May 1, 1966, p. 28.

38. Don Bodinger, interviewed by David Patten, June 17, 1999. Transcript, p. 3.

39. "History of the Bessemer Plant," Trinity Industries, news release, Jan. 23, 1995, p. 2.

40. Herb Greenberg, "Pullman Switches Off Rail Cars," *Chicago Tribune,* Oct. 1, 1983, p. 2.7.

41. Ray Wallace, interviewed by the author, Oct. 28, 1998. Transcript, p. 18.

Chapter Ten

1. "Trinity Industries Reports Earnings," PR Newswire, May 18, 1989.

2. Tim Wallace, interviewed by the author, July 13, 1999. Transcript, p. 15.

3. Elaine Belsito, "GATX," *International Directory of Company Histories,* ed. Paula Kepos, vol. 6 (Detroit: St. James Press, 1992), p. 394.

4. Ward Fuller, interviewed by the author, August 10, 1999. Transcript, p. 1.

5. Ward Fuller, interviewed by the author, August 10, 1999. Transcript, p. 1.

6. "GATX Announces New Contract With Trinity Industries," GATX Corp., news release, April 9, 1984, p. 1.

7. Tim Wallace, interviewed by the author, Oct. 28, 1998. Transcript, p. 32.

8. "GATX Announces New Contract With Trinity Industries," GATX Corp., news release, April 9, 1984, p. 2.

9. Tim Wallace, interviewed by the author, July 13, 1999. Transcript, p. 4.

10. Tim Wallace, interviewed by the author, Oct. 28, 1998. Transcript, p. 35.

11. Wally Cathcart, interviewed by Alex Lieber, June 14, 1999. Transcript, p. 14.

12. Wally Cathcart, interviewed by Alex Lieber, June 14, 1999. Transcript, p. 16.

13. Trinity Industries, Inc., news release, Jan. 9, 1995, p. 1.

14. Keith Hittle, interviewed by Alex Lieber, July 8, 1999. Transcript, p. 5.

15. Helmut Hvizdalek, interviewed by Alex Lieber, July 14, 1999. Transcript, p. 16.

16. Helmut Hvizdalek, interviewed by Alex Lieber, July 14, 1999. Transcript, p. 16.

17. Wayne Hacker, interviewed by David Patten, July 12, 1999. Transcript, p. 14.

18. Tim Wallace, interviewed by the author, Oct. 28, 1998. Transcript, p. 37.

19. Tim Wallace, interviewed by the author, Oct. 28, 1998. Transcript, p. 37.

20. Bill Neewby, interviewed by David Patten, August 20, 1999. Transcript, p. 6.

21. "Trinity Industries Buys Stemmons Tower," *Dallas Morning News,* Nov. 6, 1984, p. 4D.

22. Thomas Tucker, *International Directory of Company Histories,* ed. Paula Kepos, vol. 7 (Detroit: St. James Press, 1993), pp. 540-41.

23. Thomas Tucker, *International Directory of Company Histories,* ed. Paula Kepos, vol. 7 (Detroit: St. James Press, 1993), p. 541.

24. The Associated Press, "Closings Show Steady Fall in Shipbuilding," New Orleans *Times-Picayune*/The States-Item, Aug. 8, 1985, p. B2.

25. Ted Hughes, "Trinity Vies to Become Defense Contender," *Dallas Business Journal*, April 15, 1985, p. 1.

26. "Navy Gives Shipbuilder $85 Million Contract," New Orleans *Times-Picayune*/The States-Item, April 6, 1985, p. A35.

27. "Bell Halter Awarded Two Navy Contracts," New Orleans *Times-Picayune* Nov. 5, 1983, p. 2.4.

28. Greg Hassell, "Office Tower to Take Name of Williams," *Houston Chronicle*, May 14, 1999, Business, p. 1.

29. Judith Crown, "Steel in Eclipse: The Drying Up of Big Building Projects in Houston Has Hurt Metal Fabricators," *Houston Chronicle*, Jan. 26, 1986, Business, p. 1.

30. The Associated Press, "Pressurized Tank Maker to Close Nebraska Plant," *Tulsa World*, Jan. 15, 1986.

31. Everett A. Streit, "Successor Helped Build Moonport: Iron Works Plant Opened in 1868," *Once Upon a Time,*, vol. 1, p. 77.

32. Don Graham, interviewed by the author, Oct. 28, 1998. Transcript, p. 13.

33. "$275,000,000 Trinity Industries, Inc., Liquid Yield Option Notes due 2001," Merrill Lynch Capital Markets, Prospectus, Feb. 14, 1986, p. 8.

34. "Metal Components," Trinity Industries, Inc. 1985 Annual Report, p. 9.

35. Thomas Tucker, "Trinity Industries, Incorporated," *International Directory of Company Histories*, ed. Paula Kepos, vol. 7 (Detroit: St. James Press, 1993), p. 541.

36. Reed Abelson, et al., "Is There a Doctor in the House?: Order Breaks Out," *Forbes*, May 28, 1990, p. 262.

37. "Trinity Industries Reports Earnings," PR Newswire, May 18, 1989.

38. Ray Wallace, interviewed by the author, July 13, 1999. Transcript, p. 20.

39. Tim Wallace, interviewed by the author, July 13, 1999. Transcript, p. 21.

40. Tim Wallace, interviewed by the author, July 13, 1999. Transcript, p. 21.

41. Tim Wallace, interviewed by the author, July 13, 1999. Transcript, p. 21.

42. Tim Wallace, interviewed by the author, July 13, 1999. Transcript, p. 21.

Chapter Ten Sidebar

1. Ward Fuller, interviewed by the author, August 10, 1999. Transcript, p. 2.

2. Ward Fuller, interviewed by the author, August 10, 1999. Transcript, p. 2.

3. Ward Fuller, interviewed by the author, August 10, 1999. Transcript, p. 2.

4. Ward Fuller, interviewed by the author, August 10, 1999. Transcript, p. 15.

5. Ward Fuller, interviewed by the author, August 10, 1999. Transcript, p. 15.

Chapter Eleven

1. R. Lee Sullivan, "Nobody Else Wanted Them," *Forbes*, Oct. 10, 1994, p. 58.

2. Gary Jacobson, "The Advantages of Low-Turnover Management," *Dallas Morning News*, Jan. 15, 1995, p. H1.

3. Gary Jacobson, "The Advantages of Low-Turnover Management," *Dallas Morning News*, Jan. 15, 1995, p. H8.

4. Gary Jacobson, "The Advantages of Low-Turnover Management," *Dallas Morning News*, Jan. 15, 1995, p. H8.

5. Tim Wallace, interviewed by the author, July 13, 1999. Transcript, p. 36.

6. Howard S. Abramson, "Grain Railcar Fleet Shrinking, Experts Warn," *Journal of Commerce*, April 14, 1989, p. 1A.

7. Trinity Industries, Inc., "Announces Agreement With Ashland Oil, Inc., to Acquire Capital Stock of Beaird Industries, Inc." Southwest Newswire, January 16, 1990.

8. "UP's S.M.A.R.T. Car: First 'Show,' Then 'Tell,'" *Railway Age*, Aug. 1990, p. 16.

9. "UP's S.M.A.R.T. Car: First 'Show,' Then 'Tell,'" *Railway Age*, Aug. 1990, p. 16.

10. Steve Smith, interviewed by Alex Lieber, September 24. Taped interview.

11. "Trinity Industries, Texas Eastman Team Up on Railcar Order," joint news release, Feb. 28, 1991, p. 1.

12. "Trinity Industries, Texas Eastman Team Up on Railcar Order," joint news

release, Feb. 28, 1991, pp. 1-2.

13. "Quality Wins Award For Trinity," *Progressive Railroading*, April 1992, p. 50.

14. "Quality Wins Award For Trinity," *Progressive Railroading*, April 1992, p. 50.

15. "Trinity's QuEST Quality Enhancement Program," Trinity Industries Inc. 1993 Annual Report, p. 14.

16. "Quality Wins Award For Trinity," *Progressive Railroading*, April 1992, p. 51.

17. "Quality Wins Award For Trinity," *Progressive Railroading*, April 1992, p. 51.

18. "Quality Wins Award For Trinity," *Progressive Railroading*, April 1992, p. 51.

19. Steve Smith, interviewed by the author, July 13, 1999. Transcript, p. 20.

20. "W.R. Wallace," Texas Business Hall of Fame, 1992 videotape. Transcript, p. 3.

21. Joe Piriano, interviewed by David Patten, June 24, 1999. Transcript, p. 3.

22. Joe Piriano, interviewed by David Patten, June 24, 1999. Transcript, p. 4.

23. "Banks Receives Honors," Trinity Industries, Inc., news release, Aug. 26, 1992.

24. "Business Hall of Fame Inducts 5," *Fort Worth Star-Telegram*, Oct. 15, 1992, p. B2.

25. "W.R. Wallace," Texas Business Hall of Fame, 1992 videotape. Transcript, p. 2.

26. "W.R. Wallace," Texas Business Hall of Fame, 1992 videotape. Transcript, p. 4.

27. Dan Piller, "Railroad Picks Dallas Firm to Build 500 Jumbo Boxcars," *Fort Worth Star-Telegram*, Mar. 25, 1992.

28. David Young, "Stock Slips Despite Acquisitions, Climbing Sales," *Chicago Tribune*, Sept. 7, 1995, Business, p. 1.

29. "Plant's Troubles Began With 1980 Slump," *The Birmingham News*, April 4, 1993, p. D1.

30. "Plant's Troubles Began With 1980 Slump," *The Birmingham News*, April 4, 1993, p. D5.

31. Raymond Burton, interviewed by the author, August 10, 1999. Transcript, p. 11.

32. John Hall, "Building a Moneymaker: Shipbuilder Beats Odds With Profits," New Orleans *Times-Picayune*, Aug. 12, 1992, p. C1.

33. Gary Jacobson, "Trinity Positioned Well For Boat-Building Boom," *Dallas Morning News*, Jan. 15, 1995, p. H9.

34. Gary Jacobson, "Trinity Positioned Well For Boat-Building Boom," *Dallas Morning News*, Jan. 15, 1995, p. H9.

35. R. Lee Sullivan, "Nobody Else Wanted Them," *Forbes*, Oct. 10, 1994, p. 58.

36. John A. Jones, "Trinity Industries Speeds Up With Surge In Railcar Orders," *Investor's Business Daily*, April 15, 1993, p. 32.

37. Trinity Industries, Inc., news release, Sept. 22, 1992, p. 1.

38. Steve Stein, "Trinity Industries Buys Transit Mix Concrete," *Beaumont Enterprise*, Oct. 8, 1991, p. B3.

39. Mark Stiles, interviewed by David Patten, June 24, 1999. Transcript, p. 5.

40. Mark Stiles, interviewed by David Patten, June 24, 1999. Transcript, p. 7.

41. Mark Stiles, interviewed by David Patten, June 24, 1999. Transcript, pp. 6-7.

42. Steve Stein, "Trinity Company Buys Competitor," *Beaumont Enterprise*, Nov. 20, 1992, p. C6.

43. Robert Lenzner, "Set In Concrete," *Forbes*, July 18, 1994, p. 42.

44. Gary Jacobson, "The Advantages of Low-Turnover Management," *Dallas Morning News* Jan. 15, 1995, p. H7.

45. Manuel Castro, inteviewed by David Patten, May 23, 1999. Transcript, p. 12.

46. Ray Wallace, interviewed by Joan Thompson, September 10, 1999. Transcript, p. 3.

47. "Trinity Industries Acquisition," *The Wall Street Journal*, May 8, 1995, p. A5.

Chapter Eleven Sidebar:
The Fifth Wave

1. Walter Sutton, Jr., and David Marks, "Highways and the new wave of economic growth," U.S. Department of Transportation, July 1, 1999, No. 1, Vol. 63, p. 10.

2. "Transportation," *The New Encyclopaedia Britannica*,

Macropaedia, Chicago, Vol. 28, p. 832.

3. Lawrence H. Kaufman, "A reunion of pioneering inter-modalists," *Journal of Commerce*, August 9, 1999, Editorial/Opinion, p. 7.

4. Walter Sutton, Jr., and David Marks, "Highways and the new wave of economic growth," U.S. Department of Transportation, July 1, 1999, No. 1, Vo. 63, p. 10.

**Chapter Eleven Sidebar:
Ray Burton**

1. "Ray Burton," a TTX videotape on the history of Ray Burton. Transcript, p. 2.

2. Raymond Burton, interviewed by the author, August 10, 1999. Transcript, p. 11.

3. Raymond Burton, interviewed by the author, August 10, 1999. Transcript, p. 11.

Chapter Twelve

1. "Tribute to Ray Wallace," Trinity Industries, Inc. 1999 Annual Report, p. 4.

2. "Ray Wallace to Retire as Trinity CEO," Business Wire, July 17, 1998.

3. Jess Hay, interviewed by Joan Thompson, Feb. 2, 1998. Transcript, p. 11.

4. Tim Wallace, interviewed by the author, July 13, 1999. Transcript, p. 21.

5. Bill Neewby, interviewed by David Patten, Aug. 20, 1999. Transcript, p. 19.

6. Bill Neewby, interviewed by David Patten, Aug. 20, 1999. Transcript, p. 19.

7. Douglas Schneider, interviewed by Alex Lieber, Aug. 20, 1999. Transcript, p. 7.

8. Douglas Schneider, interviewed by Alex Lieber, Aug. 20, 1999. Transcript, p. 9.

9. "Trinity Industries Completes First Grain Cars at New Plant in Mexico," Trinity Industries Inc., news release, Feb. 6, 1998, p. 1.

10. "President of Mexico Dedicates Trinity's New Railcar Plant in Monclova, Mexico," Trinity Industries, Inc., July 2, 1998.

11. "Industrial Group," Trinity Industries, Inc. 1999 Annual Report, p. 14.

12. "International Operations & Opportunities," Trinity Industries, Inc. 1999 Annual Report, p. 16.

13. Phillip J. Longman, "Blood On the Tracks," *U.S. News & World Report*, Oct. 27, 1997, p. 52.

14. Dan Wallach, "Bigger Is Better," *Beaumont Enterprise*, May 12, 1998, p. C8.

15. Margaret Allen, "Railcar Maker Hires 200 to Meet Demand," *Dallas Business Journal*, Jan. 16, 1998, p. 1.

16. "Trinity Delivers 25,000th Railcar To GATX," Trinity Industries, Inc., news release, Oct. 15, 1998.

17. "Trinity Delivers 25,000th Railcar To GATX," Trinity Industries, Inc., news release, Oct. 15, 1998.

18. Garey Furnish, "A Very Significant Milestone," Track Crossing, newsletter, Nov. 1998, p. 8.

19. Mike Elswick, "Company Presents 25,000th Railroad Tank Car To GATX," *The Longview News-Journal*, Oct. 16, 1998.

20. Ward Fuller, interviewed by the author, Aug. 10, 1999. Transcript, p. 4.

21. Ward Fuller, interviewed by the author, Aug. 10, 1999. Transcript, pp. 4-5.

22. Steve Smith, interviewed by the author, July 13, 1999. Transcript, p. 23.

23. Wayne Hacker, interviewed by David Patten, July 12, 1999. Transcript, p. 17.

24. Don Bodinger, interviewed by David Patten, June 17, 1999. Transcript, pp. 14-15.

25. Todd Lokash, interviewed by David Patten, June 24, 1999. Transcript, pp. 4-5.

26. Ray Wallace and Timothy R. Wallace, "To Our Stockholders," Trinity Industries, Inc. 1997 Annual Report, p. 4.

27. Ray Wallace, interviewed by the author, July 13, 1999. Transcript, p. 16.

28. "Industrial Products: Metal Components Group," Trinity Industries, Inc. 1998 Annual Report, p. 14.

29. "Trinity Acquires McConway & Torley," Trinity Industries, Inc., news release, Oct. 7, 1998, p. 1.

30. John F. Stover, *American Railroads*, 2nd ed. (Chicago: U of Chicago P, 1997), pp. 140-41.

31. John H. White, Jr., *The American Railroad Freight Car* (Baltimore: The Johns Hopkins U P, 1993), p. 510.

32. John H. White Jr., *The American Railroad Freight Car* (Baltimore: The Johns Hopkins U P, 1993), p. 510.

33. "McConway & Torley Corporation," *Men and*

Women of Wartime Pittsburgh and Environs (Pittsburgh: Frank C. Harper, 1945), p. 356.

34. "McConway & Torley Corporation," *Men and Women of Wartime Pittsburgh and Environs* (Pittsburgh: Frank C. Harper, 1945), p. 356.

35. "McConway & Torley Corporation," *Men and Women of Wartime Pittsburgh and Environs* (Pittsburgh: Frank C. Harper, 1945), p. 356.

36. John Nussrallah, interviewed by the author, December 23, 1999. Transcript, p. 5.

37. Doug Schneider, interviewed by Alex Lieber, November 12, 1999. Transcript, p. 12.

38. Mark Stiles, interviewed by David Patten, December 22, 1999. Transcript, p. 5.

39. Jim Ivy, interviewed by the author, May 13, 1999. Transcript, p. 4.

40. John Adams, interviewed by Alex Lieber, December 23, 1999. Transcript, p. 5.

41. Tim Wallace, interviewed by the author, July 13, 1999. Transcript, p. 41.

42. Tim Wallace, interviewed by the author, July 13, 1999. Transcript, p. 41.

43. Mike Lintner, interviewed by the author, September 24, 1999. Transcript, p. 20.

44. Tim Wallace, interviewed by the author, July 13, 1999. Transcript, p. 41.

45. "Tribute to Ray Wallace," Trinity Industries, Inc. 1999 Annual Report, p. 4.

Chapter Twelve Sidebar: Guardrails

1. Don Graham, interviewed by the author, Oct. 28, 1998. Transcript, p. 16.

2. "Saving Time, Lives and Money ... ET2000 Improves Roadside Safety," Texas Transportation Institute, information sheet, undated.

3. "Saving Time, Lives and Money ... ET2000 Improves Roadside Safety," Texas Transportation Institute, information sheet, undated.

4. "A Partnership for Safety," Trinity Industries, Inc. 1998 Annual Report, p. 12.

Chapter Twelve Sidebar: The Right Combination

1. Matt Rose, interviewed by the author, January 17, 2000. Transcript, p. 4.

2. Matt Rose, interviewed by the author, January 17, 2000. Transcript, p. 4.

3. Matt Rose, interviewed by the author, January 17, 2000. Transcript, p. 4.

INDEX